Think Yourself Wealthy
How to Attract Riches Through Thought

Wallace D. Wattles, James Allen, & Prentice Mulford

The Science Of Getting Rich
As a Man Thinketh
Thoughts are Things

The Science of Getting Rich
by Wallace D. Wattles

Preface

This book is pragmatical, not philosophical; a practical manual, not a treatise upon theories. It is intended for the men and women whose most pressing need is for money; who wish to get rich first, and philosophize afterward. It is for those who have, so far, found neither the time, the means, nor the opportunity to go deeply into the study of metaphysics, but who want results and who are willing to take the conclusions of science as a basis for action, without going into all the processes by which those conclusions were reached.

It is expected that the reader will take the fundamental statements upon faith, just as he would take statements concerning a law of electrical action if they were promulgated by a Marconi or an Edison; and, taking the statements upon faith, that he will prove their truth by acting upon them without fear or hesitation. Every man or woman who does this will certainly get rich; for the science herein applied is an exact science, and failure is impossible. For the benefit, however, of those who wish to investigate philosophical theories and so secure a logical basis for faith, I will here cite certain authorities.

The monistic theory of the universe the theory that One is All, and that All is One; That one Substance manifests itself as the seeming many elements of the material world -is of Hindu origin, and has been gradually winning its way into the thought of the western world for two hundred years. It is the foundation of all the Oriental philosophies, and of those of Descartes, Spinoza, Leibnitz, Schopenhauer, Hegel, and Emerson.

The reader who would dig to the philosophical foundations of this is advised to read Hegel and Emerson for himself.

In writing this book I have sacrificed all other considerations to plainness and simplicity of style, so that all might understand. The plan of action laid down herein was deduced from the conclusions of philosophy; it has been thoroughly tested, and bears the supreme test of practical experiment; it works. If you wish to know how the conclusions were arrived at, read the writings of the authors mentioned above; and if you wish to reap the fruits of their philosophies in actual practice, read this book and do exactly as it tells you to do —The Author

Chapter 1: The Right To Be Rich

Whatever may be said in praise of poverty, the fact remains that it is not possible to live a really complete or successful life unless one is rich. No man can rise to his greatest possible height in talent or soul development unless he has plenty of money; for to unfold the soul and to develop talent he must have many things to use, and he cannot have these things unless he has money to buy them with.

A man develops in mind, soul, and body by making use of things, and society is so organized that man must have money in order to become the possessor of things; therefore, the basis of all advancement for man must be the science of getting rich.

The object of all life is development; and everything that lives has an inalienable right to all the development it is capable of attaining.

Man's right to life means his right to have the free and unrestricted use of all the things which may be necessary to his fullest mental, spiritual, and physical unfoldment; or, in other words, his right to be rich.

In this book, I shall not speak of riches in a figurative way; to be really rich does not mean to be satisfied or contented with a little. No man ought to be satisfied with a little if he is capable of using and enjoying more. The purpose of Nature is the advancement and unfoldment of life; and every man should have all that can contribute to the power; elegance, beauty, and richness of life; to be content with less is sinful.

The man who owns all he wants for the living of all the life he is capable of living is rich; and no man who has not plenty of money can have all he wants. Life has advanced so far, and become so complex, that even the most ordinary man or woman requires a great amount of wealth in order to live in a manner that even approaches completeness. Every person naturally wants to become all that they are capable of becoming; this desire to realize innate possibilities is inherent in human nature; we cannot help wanting to be all that we can be. Success in life is becoming what you want to be; you can become what you want to be only by making use of things, and you can have the free use of things only as you become rich enough to buy them. To understand the science of getting rich is therefore the most essential of all knowledge.

There is nothing wrong in wanting to get rich. The desire for riches is really the desire for a richer, fuller, and more abundant life; and that desire is praise worthy. The man who does not desire to live more abundantly is abnormal, and so the man who does not desire to have money enough to buy all he wants is abnormal.

There are three motives for which we live; we live for the body, we live for the mind, we live for the soul. No one of these is better or holier than the other; all are alike desirable, and no one of the three--body, mind, or soul--can live fully if either of the others is cut short of full life and expression. It is not right or noble to live only for the soul and deny mind or body; and it is wrong to live for the intellect and deny body or soul.

We are all acquainted with the loathsome consequences of living for the body and denying both mind and soul; and we see that real life means the complete expression of all that man can give forth through body, mind, and soul. Whatever he can say, no man can be really happy or satisfied unless his body is living fully in every function, and unless the same is true of his mind and his soul. Wherever there is unexpressed possibility, or function not performed, there is unsatisfied desire. Desire is possibility seeking expression, or function seeking performance.

Man cannot live fully in body without good food, comfortable clothing, and warm shelter; and without freedom from excessive toil. Rest and recreation are also necessary to his physical life.

He cannot live fully in mind without books and time to study them, without opportunity for travel and observation, or without intellectual companionship.

To live fully in mind he must have intellectual recreations, and must surround himself with all the objects of art and beauty he is capable of using and appreciating.

To live fully in soul, man must have love; and love is denied expression by poverty.

A man's highest happiness is found in the bestowal of benefits on those he loves; love finds its most natural and spontaneous expression in giving. The man who has nothing to give cannot fill his place as a husband or father, as a citizen, or as a man. It is in the use of material things that a man finds full life for his body, develops his mind, and unfolds his soul. It is therefore of supreme importance to him that he should be rich.

It is perfectly right that you should desire to be rich; if you are a normal man or woman you cannot help doing so. It is perfectly right that you should give your best attention to the Science of Getting Rich, for it is the noblest and most necessary of all studies. If you neglect this study, you are derelict in your duty to yourself, to God and humanity; for you can render to God and humanity no greater service than to make the most of yourself.

Chapter 2: There is A Science of Getting Rich

There is a Science of getting rich, and it is an exact science, like algebra or arithmetic. There are certain laws which govern the process of acquiring riches; once these laws are learned and obeyed by any man, he will get rich with mathematical certainty.

The ownership of money and property comes as a result of doing things in a certain way; those who do things in this Certain Way, whether on purpose or accidentally, get rich; while those who do not do things in this Certain Way, no matter how hard they work or how able they are, remain poor.

It is a natural law that like causes always produce like effects; and, therefore, any man or woman who learns to do things in this certain way will infallibly get rich.

That the above statement is true is shown by the following facts:

Getting rich is not a matter of environment, for, if it were, all the people in certain neighborhoods would become wealthy; the people of one city would all be rich, while those of other towns would all be poor; or the inhabitants of one state would roll in wealth, while those of an adjoining state would be in poverty.

But everywhere we see rich and poor living side by side, in the same environment, and often engaged in the same vocations. When two men are in the same locality, and in the same business, and one gets rich while the other remains poor, it shows that getting rich is not, primarily, a matter of environment. Some environments may be more favorable than others, but when two men in the same business are in the same neighborhood, and one gets rich while the other fails, it indicates that getting rich is the result of doing things in a Certain Way.

And further, the ability to do things in this certain way is not due solely to the possession of talent, for many people who have great talent remain poor, while other who have very little talent get rich.

Studying the people who have got rich, we find that they are an average lot in all respects, having no greater talents and abilities than other men. It is evident that they do not get rich because they possess talents and abilities that other men have not, but because they happen to do things in a Certain Way.

Getting rich is not the result of saving, or "thrift"; many very penurious people are poor, while free spenders often get rich.

Nor is getting rich due to doing things which others fail to do; for two men in the same business often do almost exactly the same things, and one gets rich while the other remains poor or becomes bankrupt.

From all these things, we must come to the conclusion that getting rich is the result of doing things in a Certain Way.

If getting rich is the result of doing things in a Certain Way, and if like causes always produce like effects, then any man or woman who can do things in that way can become rich, and the whole matter is brought within the domain of exact science.

The question arises here, whether this Certain Way may not be so difficult that only a few may follow it. This cannot be true, as we have seen, so far as natural ability is concerned. Talented people get rich, and blockheads get rich; intellectually brilliant people get rich, and very stupid people get rich; physically strong people get rich, and weak and sickly people get rich.

Some degree of ability to think and understand is, of course, essential; but in so far natural ability is concerned, any man or woman who has sense enough to read and understand these words can certainly get rich.

Also, we have seen that it is not a matter of environment. Location counts for something; one would not go to the heart of the Sahara and expect to do successful business. Getting rich involves the necessity of dealing with men, and of being where there are people to deal with; and if these people are inclined to deal in the way you want to deal, so much the better. But that is about as far as environment goes.

If anybody else in your town can get rich, so can you; and if anybody else in your state can get rich, so can you.

Again, it is not a matter of choosing some particular business or profession. People get rich in every business, and in every profession; while their next door neighbors in the same vocation remain in poverty.

It is true that you will do best in a business which you like, and which is congenial to you; and if you have certain talents which are well developed, you will do best in a business which calls for the exercise of those talents.

Also, you will do best in a business which is suited to your locality; an ice-cream parlor would do better in a warm climate than in Greenland, and a salmon fishery will succeed better in the Northwest than in Florida, where there are no salmon.

But, aside from these general limitations, getting rich is not dependent upon your engaging in some particular business, but upon your learning to do things in a Certain Way. If you are now in business, and anybody else in your locality is getting rich in the same business, while you are not getting rich, it is because you are not doing things in the same Way that the other person is doing them.

No one is prevented from getting rich by lack of capital. True, as you get capital the increase becomes more easy and rapid; but one who has capital is already rich, and does not need to consider how to become so. No matter how poor you may be, if you begin to do things in the Certain Way you will begin to get rich; and you will begin to have capital. The getting of capital is a part of the process of getting rich; and it is a part of the result which invariably follows the doing of things in the Certain Way. You may be the poorest man on the continent, and be deeply in debt; you may have neither friends, influence, nor resources; but if you begin to do things in this way, you must infallibly begin to get rich, for like causes must produce like effects. If you have no capital, you can get capital; if you are in the wrong business, you can get into the right business; if you are in the wrong location, you can go to the right location; and you can do so by beginning in your present business and in your present location to do things in the Certain Way which causes success.

Chapter 3: Is Opportunity Monopolized?

No man is kept poor because opportunity has been taken away from him; because other people have monopolized the wealth, and have put a fence around it. You may be shut off from engaging in business in certain lines, but there are other channels open to you. Probably it would be hard for you to get control of any of the great railroad systems; that field is pretty well monopolized. But the electric railway business is still in its infancy, and offers plenty of scope for enterprise; and it will be but a very few years until traffic and transportation through the air will become a great industry, and in all its branches will give employment to hundreds of thousands, and perhaps to millions, of people. Why not turn your attention to the development of aerial transportation, instead of competing with J.J. Hill and others for a chance in the steam railway world?

It is quite true that if you are a workman in the employ of the steel trust you have very little chance of becoming the owner of the plant in which you work; but it is also true that if you will commence to act in a Certain Way, you can soon leave the employ of the steel trust; you can buy a farm of from ten to forty acres, and engage in business as a producer of foodstuffs. There is great opportunity at this time for men who will live upon small tracts of land and cultivate the same intensively; such men will certainly get rich. You may say that it is impossible for you to get the land, but I am going to prove to you that it is not impossible, and that you can certainly get a farm if you will go to work in a Certain Way.

At different periods the tide of opportunity sets in different directions, according to the needs of the whole, and the particular stage of social evolution which has been reached. At present, in America, it is setting toward agriculture and the allied industries and professions. To-day, opportunity is open before the factory worker in his line. It is open before the business man who supplies the farmer more than before the one who supplies the factory worker; and before the professional man who waits upon the farmer more than before the one who serves the working class.

There is abundance of opportunity for the man who will go with the tide, instead of trying to swim against it.

So the factory workers, either as individuals or as a class, are not deprived of opportunity. The workers are not being "kept down" by their masters; they are not being "ground" by the trusts and combinations of capital. As a class, they are where they are because they do not do things in a Certain Way. If the workers of America chose to do so, they could follow the example of their brothers in Belgium and other countries, and establish great department stores and co-operative industries; they could elect men of their own class to office, and pass laws favoring the development of such co-operative industries; and in a few years they could take peaceable possession of the industrial field.

The working class may become the master class whenever they will begin to do things in a Certain Way; the law of wealth is the same for them as it is for all others. This they must learn; and they will remain where they are as long as they continue to do as they do. The individual worker, however, is not held down by the ignorance or the mental slothfulness of his class; he can follow the tide of opportunity to riches, and this book will tell him how.

No one is kept in poverty by a shortness in the supply of riches; there is more than enough for all. A palace as large as the capitol at Washington might be built for every family on earth from the building material in the United States alone; and under intensive cultivation, this country would produce wool, cotton, linen, and silk enough to cloth each person in the world finer than Solomon was arrayed in all his glory; together with food enough to feed them all luxuriously.

The visible supply is practically inexhaustible; and the invisible supply really is inexhaustible.

Everything you see on earth is made from one original substance, out of which all things proceed.

New Forms are constantly being made, and older ones are dissolving; but all are shapes assumed by One Thing.

There is no limit to the supply of Formless Stuff, or Original Substance. The universe is made out of it; but it was not all used in making the universe. The spaces in, through, and between the forms of the visible universe are permeated and filled with the Original Substance; with the formless Stuff; with the raw material of all things. Ten thousand times as much as has been made might still be made, and even then we should not have exhausted the supply of universal raw material.

No man, therefore, is poor because nature is poor, or because there is not enough to go around.

Nature is an inexhaustible storehouse of riches; the supply will never run short. Original Substance is alive with creative energy, and is constantly producing more forms. When the supply of building material is exhausted, more will be produced; when the soil is exhausted so that food stuffs and materials for clothing will no longer grow upon it, it will be renewed or more soil will be made. When all the gold and silver has been dug from the earth, if man is still in such a stage of social development that he needs gold and silver, more will produced from the Formless. The Formless Stuff responds to the needs of man; it will not let him be without any good thing.

This is true of man collectively; the race as a whole is always abundantly rich, and if individuals are poor, it is because they do not follow the Certain Way of doing things which makes the individual man rich.

The Formless Stuff is intelligent; it is stuff which thinks. It is alive, and is always impelled toward more life.

It is the natural and inherent impulse of life to seek to live more; it is the nature of intelligence to enlarge itself, and of consciousness to seek to extend its boundaries and find fuller expression. The universe of forms has been made by Formless Living Substance, throwing itself into form in order to express itself more fully.

The universe is a great Living Presence, always moving inherently toward more life and fuller functioning.

Nature is formed for the advancement of life; its impelling motive is the increase of life. For this cause, everything which can possibly minister to life is bountifully provided; there can be no lack unless God is to contradict himself and nullify his own works.

You are not kept poor by lack in the supply of riches; it is a fact which I shall demonstrate a little farther on that even the resources of the Formless Supply are at the command of the man or woman who will act and think in a Certain Way.

Chapter 4: The First Principle in The Science of Getting Rich

Thought is the only power which can produce tangible riches from the Formless Substance. The stuff from which all things are made is a substance which thinks, and a thought of form in this substance produces the form.

Original Substance moves according to its thoughts; every form and process you see in nature is the visible expression of a thought in Original Substance. As the Formless Stuff thinks of a form, it takes that form; as it thinks of a motion, it makes that motion. That is the way all things were created. We live in a thought world, which is part of a thought universe. The thought of a moving universe extended throughout Formless Substance, and the Thinking Stuff moving according to that thought, took the form of systems of planets, and maintains that form. Thinking Substance takes the form of its thought, and moves according to the thought. Holding the idea of a circling system of suns and worlds, it takes the form of these bodies, and moves them as it thinks. Thinking the form of a slow-growing oak tree, it moves accordingly, and produces the tree, though centuries may be required to do the work. In creating, the Formless seems to move according to the lines of motion it has established; the thought of an oak tree does not cause the instant formation of a full-grown tree, but it does start in motion the forces which will produce the tree, along established lines of growth.

Every thought of form, held in thinking Substance, causes the creation of the form, but always, or at least generally, along lines of growth and action already established.

The thought of a house of a certain construction, if it were impressed upon Formless Substance, might not cause the instant formation, of the house; but it would cause the turning of creative energies already working in trade and commerce into such channels as to result in the speedy building of the house. And if there were no existing channels through which the creative energy could work, then the house would be formed directly from primal substance, without waiting for the slow processes of the organic and inorganic world.

No thought of form can be impressed upon Original Substance without causing the creation of the form.

Man is a thinking center, and can originate thought. All the forms that man fashions with his hands must first exist in his thought; he cannot shape a thing until he has thought that thing. And so far man has confined his efforts wholly to the work of his hands; he has applied manual labor to the world of forms, seeking to change or modify those already existing. He has never thought of trying to cause the creation of new forms by impressing his thoughts upon Formless Substance.

When man has a thought-form, he takes material from the forms of nature, and makes an image of the form which is in his mind. He has, so far, made little or no effort to co-operate with Formless Intelligence; to work "with the Father." He has not dreamed that he can "do what he seeth the Father doing." Man reshapes and modifies existing forms by manual labor; he has given no attention to the question whether he may not produce things from Formless Substance by communicating his thoughts to it. We propose to prove that he may do so; to prove that any man or woman may do so, and to show how. As our first step, we must lay down three fundamental propositions.

First, we assert that there is one original formless stuff, or substance, from which all things are made. All the seemingly many elements are but different presentations of one element; all the many forms found in organic and inorganic nature are but different shapes, made from the same stuff. And this stuff is thinking stuff; a thought held in it produces the form of the thought. Thought, in thinking substance, produces shapes. Man is a thinking center, capable of original thought; if man can communicate his thought to original thinking substance, he can cause the creation, or formation, of the thing he thinks about. To summarize this:-

There is a thinking stuff from which all things are made, and which, in its original state, permeates, penetrates, and fills the interspaces of the universe.

A thought, in this substance, Produces the thing that is imaged by the thought.

Man can form things in his thought, and, by impressing his thought upon formless substance, can cause the thing he thinks about to be created.

It may be asked if I can prove these statements; and without going into details, I answer that I can do so, both by logic and experience.

Reasoning back from the phenomena of form and thought, I come to one original thinking substance; and reasoning forward from this thinking substance, I come to man's power to cause the formation of the thing he thinks about.

And by experiment, I find the reasoning true; and this is my strongest proof.

If one man who reads this book gets rich by doing what it tells him to do, that is evidence in support of my claim; but if every man who does what it tells him to do gets rich, that is positive proof until some one goes through the process and fails. The theory is true until the process fails; and this process will not fail, for every man who does exactly what this book tells him to do will get rich.

I have said that men get rich by doing things in a Certain Way; and in order to do so, men must become able to think in a certain way.

A man's way of doing things is the direct result of the way he thinks about things.

To do things in a way you want to do them, you will have to acquire the ability to think the way you want to think; this is the first step toward getting rich.

To think what you want to think is to think *Truth*, regardless of appearances.

Every man has the natural and inherent power to think what he wants to think, but it requires far more effort to do so than it does to think the thoughts which are suggested by appearances. To think according to appearance is easy; to think truth regardless of appearances is laborious, and requires the expenditure of more power than any other work man is called upon to perform.

There is no labor from which most people shrink as they do from that of sustained and consecutive thought; it is the hardest work in the world. This is especially true when truth is contrary to appearances. Every appearance in the visible world tends to produce a corresponding form in the mind which observes it; and this can only be prevented by holding the thought of the *Truth*.

To look upon the appearance of disease will produce the form of disease in your own mind, and ultimately in your body, unless you hold the thought of the truth, which is that there is no disease; it is only an appearance, and the reality is health.

To look upon the appearances of poverty will produce corresponding forms in your own mind, unless you hold to the truth that there is no poverty; there is only abundance.

To think health when surrounded by the appearances of disease, or to think riches when in the midst of appearances of poverty, requires power; but he who acquires this power becomes a *Master Mind*. He can conquer fate; he can have what he wants.

This power can only be acquired by getting hold of the basic fact which is behind all appearances; and that fact is that there is one Thinking Substance, from which and by which all things are made.

Then we must grasp the truth that every thought held in this substance becomes a form, and that man can so impress his thoughts upon it as to cause them to take form and become visible things.

When we realize this, we lose all doubt and fear, for we know that we can create what we want to create; we can get what we want to have, and can become what we want to be. As a first step toward getting rich, you must believe the three fundamental statements given previously in this chapter; and in order to emphasize them. I repeat them here:-

There is a thinking stuff from which all things are made, and which, in its original state, permeates, penetrates, and fills the interspaces of the universe.

A thought, in this substance, Produces the thing that is imaged by the thought.

Man can form things in his thought, and, by impressing his thought upon formless substance, can cause the thing he thinks about to be created.

You must lay aside all other concepts of the universe than this monistic one; and you must dwell upon this until it is fixed in your mind, and has become your habitual thought. Read these creed statements over and over again; fix every word upon your memory, and meditate upon them until you firmly believe what they say. If a doubt comes to you, cast it aside as a sin. Do not listen to arguments against this idea; do not go to churches or lectures where a contrary concept of things is taught or preached. Do not read magazines or books which teach a different idea; if you get mixed up in your faith, all your efforts will be in vain.

Do not ask why these things are true, nor speculate as to how they can be true; simply take them on trust. The science of getting rich begins with the absolute acceptance of this faith.

Chapter 5: Increasing Life

You must get rid of the last vestige of the old idea that there is a Deity whose will it is that you should be poor, or whose purposes may be served by keeping you in poverty.

The Intelligent Substance which is All, and in All, and which lives in All and lives in you, is a consciously Living Substance. Being a consciously living substance, It must have the nature and inherent desire of every living intelligence for increase of life. Every living thing must continually seek for the enlargement of its life, because life, in the mere act of living, must increase itself.

A seed, dropped into the ground, springs into activity, and in the act of living produces a hundred more seeds; life, by living, multiplies itself. It is forever Becoming More; it must do so, if it continues to be at all.

Intelligence is under this same necessity for continuous increase. Every thought we think makes it necessary for us to think another thought; consciousness is continually expanding. Every fact we learn leads us to the learning of another fact; knowledge is continually increasing. Every talent we cultivate brings to the mind the desire to cultivate another talent; we are subject to the urge of life, seeking expression, which ever drives us on to know more, to do more, and to be more.

In order to know more, do more, and be more we must have more; we must have things to use, for we learn, and do, and become, only by using things. We must get rich, so that we can live more.

The desire for riches is simply the capacity for larger life seeking fulfillment; every desire is the effort of an unexpressed possibility to come into action. It is power seeking to manifest which causes desire. That which makes you want more money is the same as that which makes the plant grow; it is Life, seeking fuller expression.

The One Living Substance must be subject to this inherent law of all life; it is permeated with the desire to live more; that is why it is under the necessity of creating things.

The One Substance desires to live more in you; hence it wants you to have all the things you can use.

It is the desire of God that you should get rich. He wants you to get rich because he can express himself better through you if you have plenty of things to use in giving him expression. He can live more in you if you have unlimited command of the means of life.

The universe desires you to have everything you want to have.

Nature is friendly to your plans.

Everything is naturally for you.

Make up your mind that this is true.

It is essential, however that your purpose should harmonize with the purpose that is in All.

You must want real life, not mere pleasure of sensual gratification. Life is the performance of function; and the individual really lives only when he performs every function, physical, mental, and spiritual, of which he is capable, without excess in any.

You do not want to get rich in order to live swinishly, for the gratification of animal desires; that is not life. But the performance of every physical function is a part of life, and no one lives completely who denies the impulses of the body a normal and healthful expression.

You do not want to get rich solely to enjoy mental pleasures, to get knowledge, to gratify ambition, to outshine others, to be famous. All these are a legitimate part of life, but the man who lives for the pleasures of the intellect alone will only have a partial life, and he will never be satisfied with his lot.

You do not want to get rich solely for the good of others, to lose yourself for the salvation of mankind, to experience the joys of philanthropy and sacrifice. The joys of the soul are only a part of life; and they are no better or nobler than any other part.

You want to get rich in order that you may eat, drink, and be merry when it is time to do these things; in order that you may surround yourself with beautiful things, see distant lands, feed your mind, and develop your intellect; in order that you may love men and do kind things, and be able to play a good part in helping the world to find truth.

But remember that extreme altruism is no better and no nobler than extreme selfishness; both are mistakes.

Get rid of the idea that God wants you to sacrifice yourself for others, and that you can secure his favor by doing so; God requires nothing of the kind.

What he wants is that you should make the most of yourself, for yourself, and for others; and you can help others more by making the most of yourself than in any other way.

You can make the most of yourself only by getting rich; so it is right and praiseworthy that you should give your first and best thought to the work of acquiring wealth.

Remember, however, that the desire of Substance is for all, and its movements must be for more life to all; it cannot be made to work for less life to any, because it is equally in all, seeking riches and life.

Intelligent Substance will make things for you, but it will not take things away from some one else and give them to you.

You must get rid of the thought of competition. You are to create, not to compete for what is already created.

You do not have to take anything away from any one.

You do not have to drive sharp bargains.

You do not have to cheat, or to take advantage. You do not need to let any man work for you for less than he earns.

You do not have to covet the property of others, or to look at it with wishful eyes; no man has anything of which you cannot have the like, and that without taking what he has away from him.

You are to become a creator, not a competitor; you are going to get what you want, but in such a way that when you get it every other man will have more than he has now.

I am aware that there are men who get a vast amount of money by proceeding in direct opposition to the statements in the paragraph above, and may add a word of explanation here. Men of the plutocratic type, who become very rich, do so sometimes purely by their extraordinary ability on the plane of competition; and sometimes they unconsciously relate themselves to Substance in its great purposes and movements for the general racial upbuilding through industrial evolution. Rockefeller, Carnegie, Morgan, et al., have been the unconscious agents of the Supreme in the necessary work of systematizing and organizing productive industry; and in the end, their work will contribute immensely toward increased life for all. Their day is nearly over; they have organized production, and will soon be succeeded by the agents of the multitude, who will organize the machinery of distribution.

The multi-millionaires are like the monster reptiles of the prehistoric eras; they play a necessary part in the evolutionary process, but the same Power which produced them will dispose of them. And it is well to bear in mind that they have never been really rich; a record of the private lives of most of this class will show that they have really been the most abject and wretched of the poor.

Riches secured on the competitive plane are never satisfactory and permanent; they are yours to-day, and another's tomorrow. Remember, if you are to become rich in a scientific and certain way, you must rise entirely out of the competitive thought. You must never think for a moment that the supply is limited. Just as soon as you begin to think that all the money is being "cornered" and controlled by bankers and others, and that you must exert yourself to get laws passed to stop this process, and so on; in that moment you drop into the competitive mind, and your power to cause creation is gone for the time being; and what is worse, you will probably arrest the creative movements you have already instituted.

Know that there are countless millions of dollars' worth of gold in the mountains of the earth, not yet brought to light; and know that if there were not, more would be created from Thinking Substance to supply your needs.

Know that the money you need will come, even if it is necessary for a thousand men to be led to the discovery of new gold mines to-morrow.

Never look at the visible supply; look always at the limitless riches in Formless Substance, and *Know* that they are coming to you as fast as you can receive and use them. Nobody, by cornering the visible supply, can prevent you from getting what is yours.

So never allow yourself to think for an instant that all the best building spots will be taken before you get ready to build your house, unless you hurry. Never worry about the trusts and combines, and get anxious for fear they will soon come to own the whole earth. Never get afraid that you will lose what you want because some other person "beats you to it." That cannot possibly happen; you are not seeking any thing that is possessed by anybody else; you are causing what you want to be created from formless Substance, and the supply is without limits. Stick to the formulated statement:--

There is a thinking stuff from which all things are made, and which, in its original state, permeates, penetrates, and fills the interspaces of the universe.

A thought, in this substance, produces the thing that is imaged by the thought.

Man can form things in his thought, and, by impressing his thought upon formless substance, can cause the thing he thinks about to be created.

Chapter 6: How Riches Come to You

When I say that you do not have to drive sharp bargains, I do not mean that you do not have to drive any bargains at all, or that you are above the necessity for having any dealings with your fellow men. I mean that you will not need to deal with them unfairly; you do not have to get something for nothing, but can give to every man more than you take from him. You cannot give every man more in cash market value than you take from him, but you can give him more in use value than the cash value of the thing you take from him. The paper, ink, and other material in this book may not be worth the money you pay for it; but if the ideas suggested by it bring you thousands of dollars, you have not been wronged by those who sold it to you; they have given you a great use value for a small cash value.

Let us suppose that I own a picture by one of the great artists, which, in any civilized community, is worth thousands of dollars. I take it to Baffin Ray, and by "salesmanship" induce an Eskimo to give a bundle of furs worth $500 for it. I have really wronged him, for he has no use for the picture; it has no use value to him; it will not add to his life.

But suppose I give him a gun worth $50 for his furs; then he has made a good bargain. He has use for the gun; it will get him many more furs and much food; it will add to his life in every way; it will make him rich.

When you rise from the competitive to the creative plane, you can scan your business transactions very strictly, and if you are selling any man anything which does not add more to his life than the thing he give you in exchange, you can afford to stop it. You do not have to beat anybody in business. And if you are in a business which does beat people, get out of it at once.

Give every man more in use value than you take from him in cash value; then you are adding to the life of the world by every business transaction.

If you have people working for you, you must take from them more in cash value than you pay them in wages; but you can so organize your business that it will be filled with the principle of advancement, and so that each employee who wishes to do so may advance a little every day.

You can make your business do for your employees what this book is doing for you. You can so conduct your business that it will be a sort of ladder, by which every employee who will take the trouble may climb to riches himself; and given the opportunity, if he will not do so it is not your fault.

And finally, because you are to cause the creation of your riches from Formless Substance which permeates all your environment, it does not follow that they are to take shape from the atmosphere and come into being before your eyes.

If you want a sewing machine, for instance, I do not mean to tell you that you are to impress the thought of a sewing machine on Thinking Substance until the machine is formed without hands, in the room where you sit, or elsewhere. But if you want a sewing machine, hold the mental image of it with the most positive certainty that it is being made, or is on its way to you. After once forming the thought, have the most absolute and unquestioning faith that the sewing machine is coming; never think of it, or speak, of it, in any other way than as being sure to arrive. Claim it as already yours.

It will be brought to you by the power of the Supreme Intelligence, acting upon the minds of men. If you live in Maine, it may be that a man will be brought from Texas or Japan to engage in some transaction which will result in your getting what you want.

If so, the whole matter will be as much to that man's advantage as it is to yours.

Do not forget for a moment that the Thinking Substance is through all, in all, communicating with all, and can influence all. The desire of Thinking Substance for fuller life and better living has caused the creation of all the sewing machines already made; and it can cause the creation of millions more, and will, whenever men set it in motion by desire and faith, and by acting in a Certain Way.

You can certainly have a sewing machine in your house; and it is just as certain that you can have any other thing or things which you want, and which you will use for the advancement of your own life and the lives of others.

You need not hesitate about asking largely; "it is your Father's pleasure to give you the kingdom," said Jesus.

Original Substance wants to live all that is possible in you, and wants you to have all that you can or will use for the living of the most abundant life.

If you fix upon your consciousness the fact that the desire you feel for the possession of riches is one with the desire of Omnipotence for more complete expression, your faith becomes invincible.

Once I saw a little boy sitting at a piano, and vainly trying to bring harmony out of the keys; and I saw that he was grieved and provoked by his inability to play real music. I asked him the cause of his vexation, and he answered, "I can feel the music in me, but I can't make my hands go right." The music in him was the *Urge* of Original Substance, containing all the possibilities of all life; all that there is of music was seeking expression through the child.

God, the One Substance, is trying to live and do and enjoy things through humanity. He is saying "I want hands to build wonderful structures, to play divine harmonies, to paint glorious pictures; I want feet to run my errands, eyes to see my beauties, tongues to tell mighty truths and to sing marvelous songs," and so on.

All that there is of possibility is seeking expression through men. God wants those who can play music to have pianos and every other instrument, and to have the means to cultivate their talents to the fullest extent; He wants those who can appreciate beauty to be able to surround themselves with beautiful things; He wants those who can discern truth to have every opportunity to travel and observe; He wants those who can appreciate dress to be beautifully clothed, and those who can appreciate good food to be luxuriously fed.

He wants all these things because it is Himself that enjoys and appreciates them; it is God who wants to play, and sing, and enjoy beauty, and proclaim truth and wear fine clothes, and eat good foods. "it is God that worketh in you to will and to do," said Paul.

The desire you feel for riches is the infinite, seeking to express Himself in you as He sought to find expression in the little boy at the piano.

So you need not hesitate to ask largely.

Your part is to focalize and express the desire to God.

This is a difficult point with most people; they retain something of the old idea that poverty and self-sacrifice are pleasing to God. They look upon poverty as a part of the plan, a necessity of nature. They have the idea that God has finished His work, and made all that He can make, and that the majority of men must stay poor because there is not enough to go around. They hold to so much of this erroneous thought that they feel ashamed to ask for wealth; they try not to want more than a very modest competence, just enough to make them fairly comfortable.

I recall now the case of one student who was told that he must get in mind a clear picture of the things he desired, so that the creative thought of them might be impressed on Formless Substance. He was a very poor man, living in a rented house, and having only what he earned from day to day; and he could not grasp the fact that all wealth was his. So, after thinking the matter over, he decided that he might reasonably ask for a new rug for the floor of his best room, and an anthracite coal stove to heat the house during the cold weather. Following the instructions given in this book, he obtained these things in a few months; and then it dawned upon him that he had not asked enough. He went through the house in which he lived, and planned all the improvements he would like to make in it; he mentally added a bay window here and a room there, until it was complete in his mind as his ideal home; and then he planned its furnishings.

Holding the whole picture in his mind, he began living in the Certain Way, and moving toward what he wanted; and he owns the house now, and is rebuilding it after the form of his mental image. And now, with still larger faith, he is going on to get greater things. It has been unto him according to his faith, and it is so with you and with all of us.

Chapter 7: Gratitude

The illustrations given in the last chapter will have conveyed to the reader the fact that the first step toward getting rich is to convey the idea of your wants to the Formless Substance.

This is true, and you will see that in order to do so it becomes necessary to relate yourself to the Formless Intelligence in a harmonious way.

To secure this harmonious relation is a matter of such primary and vital importance that I shall give some space to its discussion here, and give you instructions which, if you will follow them, will be certain to bring you into perfect unity of mind with God.

The whole process of mental adjustment and atonement can be summed up in one word, gratitude.

First, you believe that there is one Intelligent Substance, from which all things proceed; second, you believe that this Substance gives you everything you desire; and third, you relate yourself to it by a feeling of deep and profound gratitude.

Many people who order their lives rightly in all other ways are kept in poverty by their lack of gratitude. Having received one gift from God, they cut the wires which connect them with Him by failing to make acknowledgment.

It is easy to understand that the nearer we live to the source of wealth, the more wealth we shall receive; and it is easy also to understand that the soul that is always grateful lives in closer touch with God than the one which never looks to Him in thankful acknowledgment.

The more gratefully we fix our minds on the Supreme when good things come to us, the more good things we will receive, and the more rapidly they will come; and the reason simply is that the mental attitude of gratitude draws the mind into closer touch with the source from which the blessings come.

If it is a new thought to you that gratitude brings your whole mind into closer harmony with the creative energies of the universe, consider it well, and you will see that it is true. The good things you already have have come to you along the line of obedience to certain laws. Gratitude will lead your mind out along the ways by which things come; and it will keep you in close harmony with creative thought and prevent you from falling into competitive thought.

Gratitude alone can keep you looking toward the All, and prevent you from falling into the error of thinking of the supply as limited; and to do that would be fatal to your hopes.

There is a Law of Gratitude, and it is absolutely necessary that you should observe the law, if you are to get the results you seek.

The law of gratitude is the natural principle that action and reaction are always equal, and in opposite directions.

The grateful outreaching of your mind in thankful praise to the Supreme is a liberation or expenditure of force; it cannot fail to reach that to which it addressed, and the reaction is an instantaneous movement towards you.

"Draw nigh unto God, and He will draw nigh unto you." That is a statement of psychological truth.

And if your gratitude is strong and constant, the reaction in Formless Substance will be strong and continuous; the movement of the things you want will be always toward you. Notice the grateful attitude that Jesus took; how He always seems to be saying, "I thank Thee, Father, that Thou hearest me." You cannot exercise much power without gratitude; for it is gratitude that keeps you connected with Power.

But the value of gratitude does not consist solely in getting you more blessings in the future. Without gratitude you cannot long keep from dissatisfied thought regarding things as they are.

The moment you permit your mind to dwell with dissatisfaction upon things as they are, you begin to lose ground. You fix attention upon the common, the ordinary, the poor, and the squalid and mean; and your mind takes the form of these things. Then you will transmit these forms or mental images to the Formless, and the common, the poor, the squalid, and mean will come to you.

To permit your mind to dwell upon the inferior is to become inferior and to surround yourself with inferior things.

On the other hand, to fix your attention on the best is to surround yourself with the best, and to become the best.

The Creative Power within us makes us into the image of that to which we give our attention. We are Thinking Substance, and thinking substance always takes the form of that which it thinks about.

The grateful mind is constantly fixed upon the best; therefore it tends to become the best; it takes the form or character of the best, and will receive the best.

Also, faith is born of gratitude. The grateful mind continually expects good things, and expectation becomes faith. The reaction of gratitude upon one's own mind produces faith; and every outgoing wave of grateful thanksgiving increases faith. He who has no feeling of gratitude cannot long retain a living faith; and without a living faith you cannot get rich by the creative method, as we shall see in the following chapters.

It is necessary, then, to cultivate the habit of being grateful for every good thing that comes to you; and to give thanks continuously.

And because all things have contributed to your advancement, you should include all things in your gratitude.

Do not waste time thinking or talking about the shortcomings or wrong actions of plutocrats or trust magnates. Their organization of the world has made your opportunity; all you get really comes to you because of them.

Do not rage against, corrupt politicians; if it were not for politicians we should fall into anarchy, and your opportunity would be greatly lessened.

God has worked a long time and very patiently to bring us up to where we are in industry and government, and He is going right on with His work. There is not the least doubt that He will do away with plutocrats, trust magnates, captains of industry, and politicians as soon as they can be spared; but in the meantime, behold they are all very good. Remember that they are all helping to arrange the lines of transmission along which your riches will come to you, and be grateful to them all. This will bring you into harmonious relations with the good in everything, and the good in everything will move toward you.

Chapter 8: Thinking in the Certain Way

Turn back to chapter six and read again the story of the man who formed a mental image of his house, and you will get a fair idea of the initial step toward getting rich. You must form a clear and definite mental picture of what you want; you cannot transmit an idea unless you have it yourself.

You must have it before you can give it; and many people fail to impress Thinking Substance because they have themselves only a vague and misty concept of the things they want to do, to have, or to become.

It is not enough that you should have a general desire for wealth "to do good with"; everybody has that desire.

It is not enough that you should have a wish to travel, see things, live more, etc. Everybody has those desires also. If you were going to send a wireless message to a friend, you would not send the letters of the alphabet in their order, and let him construct the message for himself; nor would you take words at random from the dictionary. You would send a coherent sentence; one which meant something. When you try to impress your wants upon Substance, remember that it must be done by a coherent statement; you must know what you want, and be definite. You can never get rich, or start the creative power into action, by sending out unformed longings and vague desires.

Go over your desires just as the man I have described went over his house; see just what you want, and get a clear mental picture of it as you wish it to look when you get it.

That clear mental picture you must have continually in mind, as the sailor has in mind the port toward which he is sailing the ship; you must keep your face toward it all the time. You must no more lose sight of it than the steersman loses sight of the compass.

It is not necessary to take exercises in concentration, nor to set apart special times for prayer and affirmation, nor to "go into the silence," nor to do occult stunts of any kind. There things are well enough, but all you need is to know what you want, and to want it badly enough so that it will stay in your thoughts.

Spend as much of your leisure time as you can in contemplating your picture, but no one needs to take exercises to concentrate his mind on a thing which he really wants; it is the things you do not really care about which require effort to fix your attention upon them.

And unless you really want to get rich, so that the desire is strong enough to hold your thoughts directed to the purpose as the magnetic pole holds the needle of the compass, it will hardly be worth while for you to try to carry out the instructions given in this book.

The methods herein set forth are for people whose desire for riches is strong enough to overcome mental laziness and the love of ease, and make them work.

The more clear and definite you make your picture then, and the more you dwell upon it, bringing out all its delightful details, the stronger your desire will be; and the stronger your desire, the easier it will be to hold your mind fixed upon the picture of what you want.

Something more is necessary, however, than merely to see the picture clearly. If that is all you do, you are only a dreamer, and will have little or no power for accomplishment.

Behind your clear vision must be the purpose to realize it; to bring it out in tangible expression.

And behind this purpose must be an invincible and unwavering *faith* that the thing is already yours; that it is "at hand" and you have only to take possession of it.

Live in the new house, mentally, until it takes form around you physically. In the mental realm, enter at once into full enjoyment of the things you want.

"Whatsoever things ye ask for when ye pray, believe that ye receive them, and ye shall have them," said Jesus.

See the things you want as if they were actually around you all the time; see yourself as owning and using them. Make use of them in imagination just as you will use them when they are your tangible possessions. Dwell upon your mental picture until it is clear and distinct, and then take the Mental Attitude of Ownership toward everything in that picture. Take possession of it, in mind, in the full faith that it is actually yours. Hold to this mental ownership; do not waiver for an instant in the faith that it is real.

And remember what was said in a proceeding chapter about gratitude; be as thankful for it all the time as you expect to be when it has taken form. The man who can sincerely thank God for the things which as yet he owns only in imagination, has real faith. He will get rich; he will cause the creation of whatsoever he wants.

You do not need to pray repeatedly for things you want; it is not necessary to tell God about it every day.

"Use not vain repetitions as the heathen do," said Jesus said to his pupils, "for your Father knoweth the ye have need of these things before ye ask Him."

Your part is to intelligently formulate your desire for the things which make for a larger life, and to get these desire arranged into a coherent whole; and then to impress this Whole Desire upon the Formless Substance, which has the power and the will to bring you what you want.

You do not make this impression by repeating strings of words; you make it by holding the vision with unshakable PURPOSE to attain it, and with steadfast FAITH that you do attain it.

The answer to prayer is not according to your faith while you are talking, but according to your faith while you are working.

You cannot impress the mind of God by having a special Sabbath day set apart to tell Him what you want, and the forgetting Him during the rest of the week. You cannot impress Him by having special hours to go into your closet and pray, if you then dismiss the matter from your mind until the hour of prayer comes again.

Oral prayer is well enough, and has its effect, especially upon yourself, in clarifying your vision and strengthening your faith; but it is not your oral petitions which get you what you want. In order to get rich you do not need a "sweet hour of prayer"; you need to "pray without ceasing." And by prayer I mean holding steadily to your vision, with the purpose to cause its creation into solid form, and the faith that you are doing so.

"Believe that ye receive them."

The whole matter turns on receiving, once you have clearly formed your vision. When you have formed it, it is well to make an oral statement, addressing the Supreme in reverent prayer; and from that moment you must, in mind, receive what you ask for. Live in the new house; wear the fine clothes; ride in the automobile; go on the journey, and confidently plan for greater journeys. Think and speak of all the things you have asked for in terms of actual present ownership. Imagine an environment, and a financial condition exactly as you want them, and live all the time in that imaginary environment and financial condition. Mind, however, that you do not do this as a mere dreamer and castle builder; hold to the FAITH that the imaginary is being realized, and to the PURPOSE to realize it. Remember that it is faith and purpose in the use of the imagination which make the difference between the scientist and the dreamer. And having learned this fact, it is here that you must learn the proper use of the Will.

Chapter 9: How to Use the Will

To set about getting rich in a scientific way, you do not try to apply your will power to anything outside of yourself.

You have no right to do so, anyway.

It is wrong to apply your will to other men and women, in order to get them to do what you wish done.

It is as flagrantly wrong to coerce people by mental power as it is to coerce them by physical power. If compelling people by physical force to do things for you reduces them to slavery, compelling them by mental means accomplishes exactly the same thing; the only difference is in methods. If taking things from people by physical force is robbery, them taking things by mental force is robbery also; there is no difference in principle.

You have no right to use your will power upon another person, even "for his own good"; for you do not know what is for his good. The science of getting rich does not require you to apply power or force to any other person, in any way whatsoever. There is not the slightest necessity for doing so; indeed, any attempt to use your will upon others will only tend to defeat your purpose.

You do not need to apply your will to things, in order to compel them to come to you.

That would simply be trying to coerce God, and would be foolish and useless, as well as irreverent.

You do not have to compel God to give you good things, any more than you have to use your will power to make the sun rise.

You do not have to use your will power to conquer an unfriendly deity, or to make stubborn and rebellious forces do your bidding.

Substance is friendly to you, and is more anxious to give you what you want than you are to get it.

To get rich, you need only to use your will power upon yourself.

When you know what to think and do, then you must use your will to compel yourself to think and do the right things. That is the legitimate use of the will in getting what you want--to use it in holding yourself to the right course. Use your will to keep yourself thinking and acting in the Certain Way.

Do not try to project your will, or your thoughts, or your mind out into space, to "act" on things or people.

Keep your mind at home; it can accomplish more there than elsewhere.

Use your mind to form a mental image of what you want, and to hold that vision with faith and purpose; and use your will to keep your mind working in the Right Way.

The more steady and continuous your faith and purpose, the more rapidly you will get rich, because you will make only POSITIVE impressions upon Substance; and you will not neutralize or offset them by negative impressions.

The picture of your desires, held with faith and purpose, is taken up by the Formless, and permeates it to great distances-throughout the universe, for all I know.

As this impression spreads, all things are set moving toward its realization; every living thing, every inanimate thing, and the things yet uncreated, are stirred toward bringing into being that which you want. All force begins to be exerted in that direction; all things begin to move toward you. The minds of people, everywhere, are influenced toward doing the things necessary to the fulfilling of your desires; and they work for you, unconsciously.

But you can check all this by starting a negative impression in the Formless Substance. Doubt or unbelief is as certain to start a movement away from you as faith and purpose are to start one toward you. It is by not understanding this that most people who try to make use of "mental science" in getting rich make their failure. Every hour and moment you spend in giving heed to doubts and fears, every hour you spend in worry, every hour in which your soul is possessed by unbelief, sets a current away from you in the whole domain of intelligent Substance. All the promises are unto them that believe, and unto them only. Notice how insistent Jesus was upon this point of belief; and now you know the reason why.

Since belief is all important, it behooves you to guard your thoughts; and as your beliefs will be shaped to a very great extent by the things you observe and think about, it is important that you should command your attention.

And here the will comes into use; for it is by your will that you determine upon what things your attention shall be fixed.

If you want to become rich, you must not make a study of poverty.

Things are not brought into being by thinking about their opposites. Health is never to be attained by studying disease and thinking about disease; righteousness is not to be promoted by studying sin and thinking about sin; and no one ever got rich by studying poverty and thinking about poverty.

Medicine as a science of disease has increased disease; religion as a science of sin has promoted sin, and economics as a study of poverty will fill the world with wretchedness and want.

Do not talk about poverty; do not investigate it, or concern yourself with it. Never mind what its causes are; you have nothing to do with them.

What concerns you is the cure.

Do not spend your time in charitable work, or charity movements; all charity only tends to perpetuate the wretchedness it aims to eradicate.

I do not say that you should be hard hearted or unkind, and refuse to hear the cry of need; but you must not try to eradicate poverty in any of the conventional ways. Put poverty behind you, and put all that pertains to it behind you, and "make good."

Get rich; that is the best way you can help the poor.

And you cannot hold the mental image which is to make you rich if you fill your mind with pictures of poverty. Do not read books or papers which give circumstantial accounts of the wretchedness of the tenement dwellers, of the horrors of child labor, and so on. Do not read anything which fills your mind with gloomy images of want and suffering.

You cannot help the poor in the least by knowing about these things; and the wide-spread knowledge of them does not tend at all to do away with poverty.

What tends to do away with poverty is not the getting of pictures of poverty into your mind, but getting pictures of wealth into the minds of the poor.

You are not deserting the poor in their misery when you refuse to allow your mind to be filled with pictures of that misery.

Poverty can be done away with, not by increasing the number of well to do people who think about poverty, but by increasing the number of poor people who purpose with faith to get rich.

The poor do not need charity; they need inspiration. Charity only sends them a loaf of bread to keep them alive in their wretchedness, or gives them an entertainment to make them forget for an hour or two; but inspiration will cause them to rise out of their misery. If you want to help the poor, demonstrate to them that they can become rich; prove it by getting rich yourself.

The only way in which poverty will ever be banished from this world is by getting a large and constantly increasing number of people to practice the teachings of this book.

People must be taught to become rich by creation, not by competition.

Every man who becomes rich by competition throws down behind him the ladder by which he rises, and keeps others down; but every man who gets rich by creation opens a way for thousands to follow him, and inspires them to do so.

You are not showing hardness of heart or an unfeeling disposition when you refuse to pity poverty, see poverty, read about poverty, or think or talk about it, or to listen to those who do talk about it. Use your will power to keep your mind OFF the subject of poverty, and to keep it fixed with faith and purpose ON the vision of what you want.

Chapter 10: Further Use of the Will

You cannot retain a true and clear vision of wealth if you are constantly turning your attention to opposing pictures, whether they be external or imaginary.

Do not tell of your past troubles of a financial nature, if you have had them, do not think of them at all. Do not tell of the poverty of your parents, or the hardships of your early life; to do any of these things is to mentally class yourself with the poor for the time being, and it will certainly check the movement of things in your direction.

"Let the dead bury their dead," as Jesus said.

Put poverty and all things that pertain to poverty completely behind you.

You have accepted a certain theory of the universe as being correct, and are resting all your hopes of happiness on its being correct; and what can you gain by giving heed to conflicting theories?

Do not read religious books which tell you that the world is soon coming to an end; and do not read the writing of muck-rakers and pessimistic philosophers who tell you that it is going to the devil.

The world is not going to the devil; it is going to God.

It is wonderful Becoming.

True, there may be a good many things in existing conditions which are disagreeable; but what is the use of studying them when they are certainly passing away, and when the study of them only tends to check their passing and keep them with us? Why give time and attention to things which are being removed by evolutionary growth, when you can hasten their removal only by promoting the evolutionary growth as far as your part of it goes?

No matter how horrible in seeming may be the conditions in certain countries, sections, or places, you waste your time and destroy your own chances by considering them.

You should interest yourself in the world's becoming rich.

Think of the riches the world is coming into, instead of the poverty it is growing out of; and bear in mind that the only way in which you can assist the world in growing rich is by growing rich yourself through the creative method--not the competitive one.

Give your attention wholly to riches; ignore poverty.

Whenever you think or speak of those who are poor, think and speak of them as those who are becoming rich;as those who are to be congratulated rather than pitied. Then they and others will catch the inspiration, and begin to search for the way out.

Because I say that you are to give your whole time and mind and thought to riches, it does not follow that you are to be sordid or mean.

To become really rich is the noblest aim you can have in life, for it includes everything else. On the competitive plane, the struggle to get rich is a Godless scramble for power over other men; but when we come into the creative mind, all this is changed.

All that is possible in the way of greatness and soul unfoldment, of service and lofty endeavor, comes by way of getting rich; all is made possible by the use of things.

If you lack for physical health, you will find that the attainment of it is conditional on your getting rich.

Only those who are emancipated from financial worry, and who have the means to live a care-free existence and follow hygienic practices, can have and retain health.

Moral and spiritual greatness is possible only to those who are above the competitive battle for existence; and only those who are becoming rich on the plane of creative thought are free from the degrading influences of competition. If your heart is set on domestic happiness, remember that love flourishes best where there is refinement, a high level of thought, and freedom from corrupting influences; and these are to be found only where riches are attained by the exercise of creative thought, without strife or rivalry.

You can aim at nothing so great or noble, I repeat, as to become rich; and you must fix your attention upon your mental picture of riches, to the exclusion of all that may tend to dim or obscure the vision.

You must learn to see the underlying TRUTH in all things; you must see beneath all seemingly wrong conditions the Great One Life ever moving forward toward fuller expression and more complete happiness.

It is the truth that there is no such thing as poverty; that there is only wealth.

Some people remain in poverty because they are ignorant of the fact that there is wealth for them; and these can best be taught by showing them the way to affluence in your own person and practice.

Others are poor because, while they feel that there is a way out, they are too intellectually indolent to put forth the mental effort necessary to find that way and by travel it; and for these the very best thing you can do is to arouse their desire by showing them the happiness that comes from being rightly rich.

Others still are poor because, while they have some notion of science, they have become so swamped and lost in the maze of metaphysical and occult theories that they do not know which road to take. They try a mixture of many systems and fail in all. For these, again, the very best thing, to do is to show the right way in your own person and practice; an ounce of doing things is worth a pound of theorizing.

The very best thing you can do for the whole world is to make the most of yourself.

You can serve God and man in no more effective way than by getting rich; that is, if you get rich by the creative method and not by the competetive one.

Another thing. We assert that this book gives in detail the principles of the science of getting rich; and if that is true, you do not need to read any other book upon the subject. This may sound narrow and egotistical, but consider: there is no more scientific method of computation in mathematics than by addition, subtraction, multiplication, and division; no other method is possible. There can be but one shortest distance between two points. There is only one way to think scientifically, and that is to think in the way that leads by the most direct and simple route to the goal. No man has yet formulated a briefer or less complex "system" than the one set forth herein; it has been stripped of all non-essentials. When you commence on this, lay all others aside; put them out of your mind altogether.

Read this book every day; keep it with you; commit it to memory, and do not think about other "systems" and theories. If you do, you will begin to have doubts, and to be uncertain and wavering in your thought; and then you will begin to make failures.

After you have made good and become rich, you may study other systems as much as you please; but until you are quite sure that you have gained what you want, do not read anything on this line but this book, unless it be the authors mentioned in the Preface.

And read only the most optimistic comments on the world's news; those in harmony with your picture.

Also, postpone your investigations into the occult. Do not dabble in theosophy, Spiritualism, or kindred studies. It is very likely that the dead still live, and are near; but if they are, let them alone; mind your own business.

Wherever the spirits of the dead may be, they have their own work to do, and their own problems to solve; and we have no right to interfere with them. We cannot help them, and it is very doubtful whether they can help us, or whether we have any right to trespass upon their time if they can. Let the dead and the hereafter alone, and solve your own problem; get rich. If you begin to mix with the occult, you will start mental cross-currents which will surely bring your hopes to shipwreck. Now, this and the preceding chapters have brought us to the following statement of basic facts:--

There is a thinking stuff from which all things are made, and which, in its original state, permeates, penetrates, and fills the interspaces of the universe.

A thought, in this substance, Produces the thing that is imaged by the thought.

Man can form things in his thought, and, by impressing his thought upon formless substance, can cause the thing he thinks about to be created.

In order to do this, man must pass from the competitive to the creative mind; he must form a clear mental picture of the things he wants, and hold this picture in his thoughts with the fixed PURPOSE to get what he wants, and the unwavering FAITH that he does get what he wants, closing his mind against all that may tend to shake his purpose, dim his vision, or quench his faith.

And in addition to all this, we shall now see that he must live and act in a Certain Way.

Chapter 11: Acting in the Certain Way

Thought is the creative power, or the impelling force which causes the creative power to act; thinking in a Certain Way will bring riches to you, but you must not rely upon thought alone, paying no attention to personal action. That is the rock upon which many otherwise scientific metaphysical thinkers meet shipwreck--the failure to connect thought with personal action.

We have not yet reached the stage of development, even supposing such a stage to be possible, in which man can create directly from Formless Substance without nature's processes or the work of human hands; man must not only think, but his personal action must supplement his thought.

By thought you can cause the gold in the hearts of the mountains to be impelled toward you; but it will not mine itself, refine itself, coin itself into double eagles, and come rolling along the roads seeking its way into your pocket.

Under the impelling power of the Supreme Spirit, men's affairs will be so ordered that some one will be led to mine the gold for you; other men's business transactions will be so directed that the gold will be brought toward you, and you must so arrange your own business affairs that you may be able to receive it when it comes to you. Your thought makes all things, animate and inanimate, work to bring you what you want; but your personal activity must be such that you can rightly receive what you want when it reaches you. You are not to take it as charity, nor to steal it; you must give every man more in use value than he gives you in cash value.

The scientific use of thought consists in forming a clear and distinct mental image of what you want; in holding fast to the purpose to get what you want; and in realizing with grateful faith that you do get what you want.

Do not try to 'project' your thought in any mysterious or occult way, with the idea of having it go out and do things for you; that is wasted effort, and will weaken your power to think with sanity.

The action of thought in getting rich is fully explained in the preceding chapters; your faith and purpose positively impress your vision upon Formless Substance, which has *the same desire for more life that you have*; and this vision, received from you, sets all the creative forces at work *in and through their regular channels of action*, but directed toward you.

It is not your part to guide or supervise the creative process; all you have to do with that is to retain your vision, stick to your purpose, and maintain your faith and gratitude.

But you must act in a Certain Way, so that you can appropriate what is yours when it comes to you; so that you can meet the things you have in your picture, and put them in their proper places as they arrive.

You can really see the truth of this. When things reach you, they will be in the hands of other men, who will ask an equivalent for them.

And you can only get what is yours by giving the other man what is his.

Your pocketbook is not going to be transformed into a Fortunata's purse, which shall be always full of money without effort on your part.

This is the crucial point in the science of getting rich; right here, where thought and personal action must be combined. There are very many people who, consciously or unconsciously, set the creative forces in action by the strength and persistence of their desires, but who remain poor because they do not provide for the reception of the thing they want when it comes.

By thought, the thing you want is brought to you; by action you receive it.

Whatever your action is to be, it is evident that you must act NOW. You cannot act in the past, and it is essential to the clearness of your mental vision that you dismiss the past from your mind. You cannot act in the future, for the future is not here yet. And you cannot tell how you will want to act in any future contingency until that contingency has arrived.

Because you are not in the right business, or the right environment now, do not think that you must postpone action until you get into the right business or environment. And do not spend time in the present taking thought as to the best course in possible future emergencies; have faith in your ability to meet any emergency when it arrives.

If you act in the present with your mind on the future, your present action will be with a divided mind, and will not be effective.

Put your whole mind into present action.

Do not give your creative impulse to Original Substance, and then sit down and wait for results; if you do, you will never get them. Act now. There is never any time but now, and there never will be any time but now. If you are ever to begin to make ready for the reception of what you want, you must begin now.

And your action, whatever it is, must most likely be in your present business or employment, and must be upon the persons and things in your present environment.

You cannot act where you are not; you cannot act where you have been, and you cannot act where you are going to be; you can act only where you are.

Do not bother as to whether yesterday's work was well done or ill done; do to-day's work well. Do not try to do to-morrow's work now; there will be plenty of time to do that when you get to it.

Do not try, by occult or mystical means, to act on people or things that are out of your reach.

Do not wait for a change of environment, before you act; get a change of environment by action.

You can so act upon the environment in which you are now, as to cause yourself to be transferred to a better environment.

Hold with faith and purpose the vision of yourself in the better environment, but act upon your present environment with all your heart, and with all your strength, and with all your mind.

Do not spend any time in day dreaming or castle building; hold to the one vision of what you want, and act NOW.

Do not cast about seeking some new thing to do, or some strange, unusual, or remarkable action to perform as a first step toward getting rich. It is probable that your actions, at least for some time to come, will be those you have been performing for some time past; but you are to begin now to perform these actions in the Certain Way, which will surely make you rich.

If you are engaged in some business, and feel that it is not the right one for you, do not wait until you get into the right business before you begin to act.

Do not feel discouraged, or sit down and lament because you are misplaced. No man was ever so misplaced but that he could not find the right place, and no man ever became so involved in the wrong business but that he could get into the right business.

Hold the vision of yourself in the right business, with the purpose to get into it, and the faith that you will get into it, and are getting into it; but ACT in your present business. Use your present business as the means of getting a better one, and use your present enviornment as the means of getting into a better one. Your vision of the right business, if held with faith and purpose, will cause the Supreme to move the right business toward you; and your action, if performed in the Certain Way, will cause you to move toward the business.

If you are an employee, or wage earner, and feel that you must change places in order to get what you want, do not 'project" your thought into space and rely upon it to get you another job. It will probably fail to do so.

Hold the vision of yourself in the job you want, while you ACT with faith and purpose on the job you have, and you will certainly get the job you want.

Your vision and faith will set the creative force in motion to bring it toward you, and your action will cause the forces in your own environment to move you toward the place you want. In closing this chapter, we will add another statement to our syllabus:--

There is a thinking stuff from which all things are made, and which, in its original state, permeates, penetrates, and fills the interspaces of the universe.

A thought, in this substance, Produces the thing that is imaged by the thought.

Man can form things in his thought, and, by impressing his thought upon formless substance, can cause the thing he thinks about to be created.

In order to do this, man must pass from the competitive to the creative mind; he must form a clear mental picture of the things he wants, and hold this picture in his thoughts with the fixed *Purpose* to get what he wants, and the unwavering *Faith* that he does get what he wants, closing his mind to all that may tend to shake his purpose, dim his vision, or quench his faith.

That he may receive what he wants when it comes, man must act *Now* upon the people and things in his present environment.

Chapter 12: Efficient Action

You must use your thought as directed in previous chapters, and begin to do what you can do where you are; and you must do ALL that you can do where you are.

You can advance only be being larger than your present place; and no man is larger than his present place who leaves undone any of the work pertaining to that place.

The world is advanced only by those who more than fill their present places.

If no man quite filled his present place, you can see that there must be a going backward in everything. Those who do not quite fill their present places are dead weight upon society, government, commerce, and industry; they must be carried along by others at a great expense. The progress of the world is retarded only by those who do not fill the places they are holding; they belong to a former age and a lower stage or plane of life, and their tendency is toward degeneration. No society could advance if every man was smaller than his place; social evolution is guided by the law of physical and mental evolution. In the animal world, evolution is caused by excess of life.

When an organism has more life than can be expressed in the functions of its own plane, it develops the organs of a higher plane, and a new species is originated.

There never would have been new species had there not been organisms which more than filled their places. The law is exactly the same for you; your getting rich depends upon your applying this principle to your own affairs.

Every day is either a successful day or a day of failure; and it is the successful days which get you what you want. If everyday is a failure, you can never get rich; while if every day is a success, you cannot fail to get rich.

If there is something that may be done today, and you do not do it, you have failed in so far as that thing is concerned; and the consequences may be more disastrous than you imagine.

You cannot foresee the results of even the most trivial act; you do not know the workings of all the forces that have been set moving in your behalf. Much may be depending on your doing some simple act; it may be the very thing which is to open the door of opportunity to very great possibilities. You can never know all the combinations which Supreme Intelligence is making for you in the world of things and of things and of human affairs; your neglect or failure to do some small thing may cause a long delay in getting what you want.

Do, every day, ALL that can be done that day.

There is, however, a limitation or qualification of the above that you must take into account.

You are not to overwork, nor to rush blindly into your business in the effort to do the greatest possible number of things in the shortest possible time.

You are not to try to do tomorrow's work today, nor to do a week's work in a day.

It is really not the number of things you do, but the *efficiency* of each separate action that counts.

Every act is, in itself, either a success or a failure.

Every act is, in itself, either effective or inefficient.

Every inefficient act is a failure, and if you spend your life in doing inefficient acts, your whole life will be a failure.

The more things you do, the worse for you, if all your acts are inefficient ones.

On the other hand, every efficient act is a success in itself, and if every act of your life is an efficient one, your whole life *must* be a success.

The cause of failure is doing too many things in an inefficient manner, and not doing enough things in an efficient manner.

You will see that it is a self-evident proposition that if you do not do any inefficient acts, and if you do a sufficient number of efficient acts, you will become rich. If, now, it is possible for you to make each act an efficient one, you see again that the getting of riches is reduced to an exact science, like mathematics.

The matter turns, then, on the questions whether you can make each separate act a success in itself. And this you can certainly do.

You can make each act a success, because *all* Power is working with you; and ALL Power cannot fail.

Power is at your service; and to make each act efficient you have only to put power into it.

Every action is either strong or weak; and when every one is strong, you are acting in the Certain Way which will make you rich.

Every act can be made strong and efficient by holding your vision while you are doing it, and putting the whole power of your *faith* and *purpose* into it.

It is at this point that the people fail who separate mental power from personal action. They use the power of mind in one place and at one time, and they act in another pace and at another time. So their acts are not successful in themselves; too many of them are inefficient. But if *all* Power goes into every act, no matter how commonplace, every act will be a success in itself; and as in the nature of things every success opens the way to other successes, your progress toward what you want, and the progress of what you want toward you, will become increasingly rapid.

Remember that successful action is cumulative in its results. Since the desire for more life is inherent in all things, when a man begins to move toward larger life more things attach themselves to him, and the influence of his desire is multiplied.

Do, every day, all that you can do that day, and do each act in an efficient manner.

In saying that you must hold your vision while you are doing each act, however trivial or commonplace, I do not mean to say that it is necessary at all times to see the vision distinctly to its smallest details. It should be the work of your leisure hours to use your imagination on the details of your vision, and to contemplate them until they are firmly fixed upon memory. If you wish speedy results, spend practically all your spare time in this practice.

By continuous contemplation you will get the picture of what you want, even to the smallest details, so firmly fixed upon your mind, and so completely transferred to the mind of Formless Substance, that in your working hours you need only to mentally refer to the picture to stimulate your faith and purpose, and cause your best effort to be put forth. Contemplate your picture in your leisure hours until your consciousness is so full of it that you can grasp it instantly. You will become so enthused with its bright promises that the mere thought of it will call forth the strongest energies of your whole being.

Let us again repeat our syllabus, and by slightly changing the closing statements bring it to the point we have now reached.

There is a thinking stuff from which all things are made, and which, in its original state, permeates, penetrates, and fills the interspaces of the universe.

A thought, in this substance, Produces the thing that is imaged by the thought.

Man can form things in his thought, and, by impressing his thought upon formless substance, can cause the thing he thinks about to be created.

In order to do this, man must pass from the competitive to the creative mind; he must form a clear mental picture of the things he wants, and do, with faith and purpose, all that can be done each day, doing each separate thing in an efficient manner.

Chapter 13: Getting into the Right Business

Success, in any particular business, depends for one thing upon your possessing in a well-developed state the faculties required in that business.

Without good musical faculty no one can succeed as a teacher of music; without well-developed mechanical faculties no one can achieve great success in any of the mechanical trades; without tact and the commercial faculties no one can succeed in mercantile pursuits. But to possess in a well-developed state the faculties required in your particular vocation does not insure getting rich. There are musicians who have remarkable talent, and who yet remain poor; there are blacksmiths, carpenters, and so on who have excellent mechanical ability, but who do not get rich; and there are merchants with good faculties for dealing with men who nevertheless fail.

The different faculties are tools; it is essential to have good tools, but it is also essential that the tools should be used in the Right Way. One man can take a sharp saw, a square, a good plane, and so on, and build a handsome article of furniture; another man can take the same tools and set to work to duplicate the article, but his production will be a botch. He does not know how to use good tools in a successful way.

The various faculties of your mind are the tools with which you must do the work which is to make you rich; it will be easier for you to succeed if you get into a business for which you are well equipped with mental tools.

Generally speaking, you will do best in that business which will use your strongest faculties; the one for which you are naturally "best fitted." But there are limitations to this statement, also. No man should regard his vocation as being irrevocably fixed by the tendencies with which he was born.

You can get rich in *Any* business, for if you have not the right talent for you can develop that talent; it merely means that you will have to make your tools as you go along, instead of confining yourself to the use of those with which you were born. It will be *Easier* for you to succeed in a vocation for which you already have the talents in a well-developed state; but you *Can* succeed in any vocation, for you can develop any rudimentary talent, and there is no talent of which you have not at least the rudiment.

You will get rich most easily in point of effort, if you do that for which you are best fitted; but you will get rich most satisfactorily if you do that which you *want* to do.

Doing what you want to do is life; and there is no real satisfaction in living if we are compelled to be forever doing something which we do not like to do, and can never do what we want to do. And it is certain that you can do what you want to do; the desire to do it is proof that you have within you the power which can do it.

Desire is a manifestation of power.

The desire to play music is the power which can play music seeking expression and development; the desire to invent mechanical devices is the mechanical talent seeking expression and development.

Where there is no power, either developed or undeveloped, to do a thing, there is never any desire to do that thing; and where there is strong desire to do a thing, it is certain proof that the power to do it is strong, and only requires to be developed and applied in the Right Way.

All things else being equal, it is best to select the business for which you have the best developed talent; but if you have a strong desire to engage in any particular line of work, you should select that work as the ultimate end at which you aim.

You can do what you want to do, and it is your right and privilege to follow the business or avocation which will be most congenial and pleasant.

You are not obliged to do what you do not like to do, and should not do it except as a means to bring you to the doing of the thing you want to do.

If there are past mistakes whose consequences have placed you in an undesirable business or environment, you may be obliged for some time to do what you do not like to do; but you can make the doing of it pleasant by knowing that it is making it possible for you to come to the doing of what you want to do.

If you feel that you are not in the right vocation, do not act too hastily in trying to get into another one. The best way, generally, to change business or environment is by growth.

Do not be afraid to make a sudden and radical change if the opportunity is presented, and you feel after careful consideration that it is the right opportunity; but never take sudden or radical action when you are in doubt as to the wisdom of doing so.

There is never any hurry on the creative plane; and there is no lack of opportunity.

When you get out of the competitive mind you will understand that you never need to act hastily. No one else is going to beat you to the thing you want to do; there is enough for all. If one space is taken, another and a better one will be opened for you a little farther on; there is plenty of time. When you are in doubt, wait. Fall back on the contemplation of your vision, and increase your faith and purpose; and by all means, in times of doubt and indecision, cultivate gratitude.

A day or two spent in contemplating the vision of what you want, and in earnest thanksgiving that you are getting it, will bring your mind into such close relationship with the Supreme that you will make no mistake when you do act.

There is a mind which knows all there is to know; and you can come into close unity with this mind by faith and the purpose to advance in life, if you have deep gratitude.

Mistakes come from acting hastily, or from acting in fear or doubt, or in forgetfulness of the Right Motive, which is more life to all, and less to none.

As you go on in the Certain Way, opportunities will come to you in increasing number; and you will need to be very steady in your faith and purpose, and to keep in close touch with the All Mind by reverent gratitude.

Do all that you can do in a perfect manner every day, but do it without haste, worry, or fear. Go as fast as you can, but never hurry.

Remember that in the moment you begin to hurry you cease to be a creator and become a competitor; you drop back upon the old plane again.

Whenever you find yourself hurrying, call a halt; fix your attention on the mental image of the thing you want, and begin to give thanks that you are getting it. The exercise of *gratitude* will never fail to strengthen your faith and renew your purpose.

Chapter 14: The Impression of Increase

Whether you change your vocation or not, your actions for the present must be those pertaining to the business in which you are now engaged.

You can get into the business you want by making constructive use of the business you are already established in; by doing your daily work in a Certain Way.

And in so far as your business consists in dealing with other men, whether personally or by letter, the key-thought of all your efforts must be to convey to their minds the impression of increase.

Increase is what all men and all women are seeking; it is the urge of the Formless Intelligence within them, seeking fuller expression.

The desire for increase is inherent in all nature; it is the fundamental impulse of the universe. All human activities are based on the desire for increase; people are seeking more food, more clothes, better shelter, more luxury, more beauty, more knowledge, more pleasure-- increase in something, more life.

Every living thing is under this necessity for continuous advancement; where increase of life ceases, dissolution and death set in at once.

Man instinctively knows this, and hence he is forever seeking more. This law of perpetual increase is set forth by Jesus in the parable of the talents; only those who gain more retain any; from him who hath not shall be taken away even that which he hath.

The normal desire for increased wealth is not an evil or a reprehensible thing; it is simply the desire for more abundant life; it is aspiration.

And because it is the deepest instinct of their natures, all men and women are attracted to him who can give them more of the means of life.

In following the Certain Way as described in the foregoing pages, you are getting continuous increase for yourself, and you are giving it to all with whom you deal.

You are a creative center, from which increase is given off to all.

Be sure of this, and convey assurance of the fact to every man, woman, and child with whom you come in contact. No matter how small the transaction, even if it be only the selling of a stick of candy to a little child, put into it the thought of increase, and make sure that the customer is impressed with the thought.

Convey the impression of advancement with everything you do, so that all people shall receive the impression that you are an Advancing Man, and that you advance all who deal with you. Even to the people whom you meet in a social way, without any thought of business, and to whom you do not try to sell anything, give the thought of increase.

You can convey this impression by holding the unshakable faith that you, yourself, are in the Way of Increase; and by letting this faith inspire, fill, and permeate every action.

Do everything that you do in the firm conviction that you are an advancing personality, and that you are giving advancement to everybody.

Feel that you are getting rich, and that in so doing you are making others rich, and conferring benefits on all.

Do not boast or brag of your success, or talk about it unnecessarily; true faith is never boastful.

Wherever you find a boastful person, you find one who is secretly doubtful and afraid. Simply feel the faith, and let it work out in every transaction; let every act and tone and look express the quiet assurance that you are getting rich; that you are already rich. Words will not be necessary to communicate this feeling to others; they will feel the sense of increase when in your presence, and will be attracted to you again.

You must so impress others that they will feel that in associating with you they will get increase for themselves. See that you give them a use value greater than the cash value you are taking from them.

Take an honest pride in doing this, and let everybody know it; and you will have no lack of customers. People will go where they are given increase; and the Supreme, which desires increase in all, and which knows all, will move toward you men and women who have never heard of you. Your business will increase rapidly, and you will be surprised at the unexpected benefits which will come to you. You will be able from day to day to make larger combinations, secure greater advantages, and to go on into a more congenial vocation if you desire to do so.

But in doing all this, you must never lose sight of your vision of what you want, or your faith and purpose to get what you want.

Let me here give you another word of caution in regard to motives.

Beware of the insidious temptation to seek for power over other men.

Nothing is so pleasant to the unformed or partially developed mind as the exercise of power or dominion over others. The desire to rule for selfish gratification has been the curse of the world. For countless ages kings and lords have drenched the earth with blood in their battles to extend their dominions; this not to seek more life for all, but to get more power for themselves.

To-day, the main motive in the business and industrial world is the same; men marshal their armies of dollars, and lay waste the lives and hearts of millions in the same mad scramble for power over others. Commercial kings, like political kings, are inspired by the lust for power.

Jesus saw in this desire for mastery the moving impulse of that evil world He sought to overthrow. Read the twenty-third chapter of Matthew, and see how He pictures the lust of the Pharisees to be called "Master," to sit in the high places, to domineer over others, and to lay burdens on the backs of the less fortunate; and note how He compares this lust for dominion with the brotherly seeking for the Common Good to which He calls His disciples.

Look out for the temptation to seek for authority, to become a "master," to be considered as one who is above the common herd, to impress others by lavish display, and so on.

The mind that seeks for mastery over others is the competitive mind; and the competitive mind is not the creative one. In order to master your environment and your destiny, it is not at all necessary that you should rule over your fellow men and indeed, when you fall into the world's struggle for the high places, you begin to be conquered by fate and environment, and your getting rich becomes a matter of chance and speculation.

Beware of the competitive mind!! No better statement of the principle of creative action can be formulated than the favorite declaration of the late "Golden Rule" Jones of Toledo: "What I want for myself, I want for everybody."

Chapter 15: The Advancing Man

What I have said in the last chapter applies as well to the professional man and the wage-earner as to the man who is engaged in mercantile business.

No matter whether you are a physician, a teacher, or a clergyman, if you can give increase of life to others and make them sensible of the fact, they will be attracted to you, and you will get rich. The physician who holds the vision of himself as a great and successful healer, and who works toward the complete realization of that vision with faith and purpose, as described in former chapters, will come into such close touch with the Source of Life that he will be phenomenally successful; patients will come to him in throngs.

No one has a greater opportunity to carry into effect the teaching of this book than the practitioner of medicine; it does not matter to which of the various schools he may belong, for the principle of healing is common to all of them, and may be reached by all alike. The Advancing Man in medicine, who holds to a clear mental image of himself as successful, and who obeys the laws of faith, purpose, and gratitude, will cure every curable case he undertakes, no matter what remedies he may use.

In the field of religion, the world cries out for the clergyman who can teach his hearers the true science of abundant life. He who masters the details of the science of getting rich, together with the allied sciences of being well, of being great, and of winning love, and who teaches these details from the pulpit, will never lack for a congregation. This is the gospel that the world needs; it will give increase of life, and men will hear it gladly, and will give liberal support to the man who brings it to them.

What is now needed is a demonstration of the science of life from the pulpit. We want preachers who can not only tell us how, but who in their own persons will show us how. We need the preacher who will himself be rich, healthy, great, and beloved, to teach us how to attain to these things; and when he comes he will find a numerous and loyal following.

The same is true of the teacher who can inspire the children with the faith and purpose of the advancing life. He will never be "out of a job." And any teacher who has this faith and purpose can give it to his pupils; he cannot help giving it to them if it is part of his own life and practice.

What is true of the teacher, preacher, and physician is true of the lawyer, dentist, real estate man, insurance agent--of everybody.

The combined mental and personal action I have described is infallible; it cannot fail. Every man and woman who follows these instructions steadily, perseveringly, and to the letter, will get rich. The law of the Increase of Life is as mathematically certain in its operation as the law of gravitation; getting rich is an exact science.

The wage-earner will find this as true of his case as of any of the others mentioned. Do not feel that you have no chance to get rich because you are working where there is no visible opportunity for advancement, where wages are small and the cost of living high. Form your clear mental vision of what you want, and begin to act with faith and purpose.

Do all the work you can do, every day, and do each piece of work in a perfectly successful manner; put the power of success, and the purpose to get rich, into everything that you do.

But do not do this merely with the idea of currying favor with your employer, in the hope that he, or those above you, will see your good work and advance you; it is not likely that they will do so.

The man who is merely a "good" workman, filling his place to the very best of his ability, and satisfied with that, is valuable to his employer; and it is not to the employer's interest to promote him; he is worth more where he is.

To secure advancement, something more is necessary than to be too large for your place.

The man who is certain to advance is the one who is too big for his place, and who has a clear concept of what he wants to be; who knows that he can become what he wants to be and who is determined to BE what he wants to be.

Do not try to more than fill your present place with a view to pleasing your employer; do it with the idea of advancing yourself. Hold the faith and purpose of increase during work hours, after work hours, and before work hours. Hold it in such a way that every person who comes in contact with you, whether foreman, fellow workman, or social acquaintance, will feel the power of purpose radiating from you; so that every one will get the sense of advancement and increase from you. Men will be attracted to you, and if there is no possibility for advancement in your present job, you will very soon see an opportunity to take another job.

There is a Power which never fails to present opportunity to the Advancing Man who is moving in obedience to law.

God cannot help helping you, if you act in a Certain Way; He must do so in order to help Himself.

There is nothing in your circumstances or in the industrial situation that can keep you down. If you cannot get rich working for the steel trust, you can get rich on a ten-acre farm; and if you begin to move in the Certain Way, you will certainly escape from the "clutches" of the steel trust and get on to the farm or wherever else you wish to be.

If a few thousands of its employees would enter upon the Certain Way, the steel trust would soon be in a bad plight; it would have to give its workingmen more opportunity, or go out of business. Nobody has to work for a trust; the trusts can keep men in so called hopeless conditions only so long as there are men who are too ignorant to know of the science of getting rich, or too intellectually slothful to practice it.

Begin this way of thinking and acting, and your faith and purpose will make you quick to see any opportunity to better your condition.

Such opportunities will speedily come, for the Supreme, working in All, and working for you, will bring them before you.

Do not wait for an opportunity to be all that you want to be; when an opportunity to be more than you are now is presented and you feel impelled toward it, take it. It will be the first step toward a greater opportunity.

There is no such thing possible in this universe as a lack of opportunities for the man who is living the advancing life.

It is inherent in the constitution of the cosmos that all things shall be for him and work together for his good; and he must certainly get rich if he acts and thinks in the Certain Way. So let wage-earning men and women study this book with great care, and enter with confidence upon the course of action it prescribes; it will not fail.

Chapter 16: Some Cautions, and Concluding Observations

Many people will scoff at the idea that there is an exact science of getting rich; holding the impression that the supply of wealth is limited, they will insist that social and governmental institutions must be changed before even any considerable number of people can acquire a competence.

But this is not true.

It is true that existing governments keep the masses in poverty, but this is because the masses do not think and act in the Certain Way.

If the masses begin to move forward as suggested in this book, neither governments nor industrial systems can check them; all systems must be modified to accommodate the forward movement.

If the people have the Advancing Mind, have the Faith that they can become rich, and move forward with the fixed purpose to become rich, nothing can possibly keep them in poverty.

Individuals may enter upon the Certain Way at any time, and under any government, and make themselves rich; and when any considerable number of individuals do so under any government, they will cause the system to be so modified as to open the way for others.

The more men who get rich on the competitive plane, the worse for others; the more who get rich on the creative plane, the better for others.

The economic salvation of the masses can only be accomplished by getting a large number of people to practice the scientific method set down in this book, and become rich. These will show others the way, and inspire them with a desire for real life, with the faith that it can be attained, and with the purpose to attain it.

For the present, however, it is enough to know that neither the government under which you live nor the capitalistic or competitive system of industry can keep you from getting rich. When you enter upon the creative plane of thought you will rise above all these things and become a citizen of another kingdom.

But remember that your thought must be held upon the creative plane; you are never for an instant to be betrayed into regarding the supply as limited, or into acting on the moral level of competition.

Whenever you do fall into old ways of thought, correct yourself instantly; for when you are in the competitive mind, you have lost the cooperation of the Mind of the Whole.

Do not spend any time in planning as to how you will meet possible emergencies in the future, except as the necessary policies may affect your actions today. You are concerned with doing today's work in a perfectly successful manner, and not with emergencies which may arise tomorrow; you can attend to them as they come.

Do not concern yourself with questions as to how you shall surmount obstacles which may loom upon your business horizon, unless you can see plainly that your course must be altered today in order to avoid them.

No matter how tremendous an obstruction may appear at a distance, you will find that if you go on in the Certain Way it will disappear as you approach it, or that a way over, through, or around it will appear.

No possible combination of circumstances can defeat a man or woman who is proceeding to get rich along strictly scientific lines. No man or woman who obeys the law can fail to get rich, any more than one can multiply two by two and fail to get four.

Give no anxious thought to possible disasters, obstacles, panics, or unfavorable combinations of circumstances; it is time enough to meet such things when they present themselves before you in the immediate present, and you will find that every difficulty carries with it the wherewithal for its overcoming.

Guard your speech. Never speak of yourself, your affairs, or of anything else in a discouraged or discouraging way.

Never admit the possibility of failure, or speak in a way that infers failure as a possibility.

Never speak of the times as being hard, or of business conditions as being doubtful. Times may be hard and business doubtful for those who are on the competitive plane, but they can never be so for you; you can create what you want, and you are above fear.

When others are having hard times and poor business, you will find your greatest opportunities.

Train yourself to think of and to look upon the world as a something which is Becoming, which is growing; and to regard seeming evil as being only that which is undeveloped. Always speak in terms of advancement; to do otherwise is to deny your faith, and to deny your faith is to lose it.

Never allow yourself to feel disappointed. You may expect to have a certain thing at a certain time, and not get it at that time; and this will appear to you like failure.

But if you hold to your faith you will find that the failure is only apparent.

Go on in the certain way, and if you do not receive that thing, you will receive something so much better that you will see that the seeming failure was really a great success.

A student of this science had set his mind on making a certain business combination which seemed to him at the time to be very desirable, and he worked for some, weeks to bring it about. When the crucial time came, the thing failed in a perfectly inexplicable way; it was as if some unseen influence had been working secretly against him. He was not disappointed; on the contrary, he thanked God that his desire had been overruled, and went steadily on with a grateful mind. In a few weeks an opportunity so much better came his way that he would not have made the first deal on any account; and he saw that a Mind which knew more than he knew had prevented him from losing the greater good by entangling himself with the lesser.

That is the way every seeming failure will work out for you, if you keep your faith, hold to your purpose, have gratitude, and do, every day, all that can be done that day, doing each separate act in a successful manner.

When you make a failure, it is because you have not asked for enough; keep on, and a larger thing then you were seeking will certainly come to you. Remember this.

You will not fail because you lack the necessary talent to do what you wish to do. If you go on as I have directed, you will develop all the talent that is necessary to the doing of your work.

It is not within the scope of this book to deal with the science of cultivating talent; but it is as certain and simple as the process of getting rich.

However, do not hesitate or waver for fear that when you come to any certain place you will fail for lack of ability; keep right on, and when you come to that place, the ability will be furnished to you. The same source of Ability which enabled the untaught Lincoln to do the greatest work in government ever accomplished by a single man is open to you; you may draw upon all the mind there is for wisdom to use in meeting the responsibilities which are laid upon you. Go on in full faith.

Study this book. Make it your constant companion until you have mastered all the ideas contained in it. While you are getting firmly established in this faith, you will do well to give up most recreations and pleasure; and to stay away from places where ideas conflicting with these are advanced in lectures or sermons. Do not read pessimistic or conflicting literature, or get into arguments upon the matter. Do very little reading, outside of the writers mentioned in the Preface. Spend most of your leisure time in contemplating your vision, and in cultivating gratitude, and in reading this book. It contains all you need to know of the science of getting rich; and you will find all the essentials summed up in the following chapter.

Chapter 17: Summary of the Science of Getting Rich

There is a thinking stuff from which all things are made, and which, in its original state, permeates, penetrates, and fills the interspaces of the universe.

A thought in this substance produces the thing that is imaged by the thought.

Man can form things in his thought, and by impressing his thought upon formless substance can cause the thing he thinks about to be created.

In order to do this, man must pass from the competitive to the creative mind; otherwise he cannot be in harmony with the Formless Intelligence, which is always creative and never competitive in spirit.

Man may come into full harmony with the Formless Substance by entertaining a lively and sincere gratitude for the blessings it bestows upon him. Gratitude unifies the mind of man with the intelligence of Substance, so that man's thoughts are received by the Formless. Man can remain upon the creative plane only by uniting himself with the Formless Intelligence through a deep and continuous feeling of gratitude.

Man must form a clear and definite mental image of the things he wishes to have, to do, or to become; and he must hold this mental image in his thoughts, while being deeply grateful to the Supreme that all his desires are granted to him. The man who wishes to get rich must spend his leisure hours in contemplating his Vision, and in earnest thanksgiving that the reality is being given to him. Too much stress cannot be laid on the importance of frequent contemplation of the mental image, coupled with unwavering faith and devout gratitude. This is the process by which the impression is given to the Formless, and the creative forces set in motion.

The creative energy works through the established channels of natural growth, and of the industrial and social order. All that is included in his mental image will surely be brought to the man who follows the instructions given above, and whose faith does not waver. What he wants will come to him through the ways of established trade and commerce.

In order to receive his own when it shall come to him, man must be active; and this activity can only consist in more than filling his present place. He must keep in mind the Purpose to get rich through the realization of his mental image. And he must do, every day, all that can be done that day, taking care to do each act in a successful manner. He must give to every man a use value in excess of the cash value he receives, so that each transaction makes for more life; and he must so hold the Advancing Thought that the impression of increase will be communicated to all with whom he comes in contact.

The men and women who practice the foregoing instructions will certainly get rich; and the riches they receive will be in exact proportion to the definiteness of their vision, the fixity of their purpose, the steadiness of their faith, and the depth of their gratitude.

As a Man Thinketh
by James Allen

Mind is the Master power that moulds and makes,
And Man is Mind, and evermore he takes
The tool of Thought, and, shaping what he wills,
Brings forth a thousand joys, a thousand ills:—
He thinks in secret, and it comes to pass:
Environment is but his looking-glass.

FOREWORD

THIS little volume (the result of meditation and experience) is not intended as an exhaustive treatise on the much-written-upon subject of the power of thought. It is suggestive rather than explanatory, its object being to stimulate men and women to the discovery and perception of the truth that—

"They themselves are makers of themselves."

by virtue of the thoughts, which they choose and encourage; that mind is the master-weaver, both of the inner garment of character and the outer garment of circumstance, and that, as they may have hitherto woven in ignorance and pain they may now weave in enlightenment and happiness.

James Allen.
Broad Park Avenue,
Ilfracombe,
England

THOUGHT AND CHARACTER

The aphorism, "As a man thinketh in his heart so is he," not only embraces the whole of a man's being, but is so comprehensive as to reach out to every condition and circumstance of his life. A man is literally *what he thinks*, his character being the complete sum of all his thoughts.

As the plant springs from, and could not be without, the seed, so every act of a man springs from the hidden seeds of thought, and could not have appeared without them. This applies equally to those acts called "spontaneous" and "unpremeditated" as to those, which are deliberately executed.

Act is the blossom of thought, and joy and suffering are its fruits; thus does a man garner in the sweet and bitter fruitage of his own husbandry.

"Thought in the mind hath made us, What we are By thought was wrought and built. If a man's mind Hath evil thoughts, pain comes on him as comes The wheel the ox behind....

..If one endure In purity of thought, joy follows him As his own shadow—sure."

Man is a growth by law, and not a creation by artifice, and cause and effect is as absolute and undeviating in the hidden realm of thought as in the world of visible and material things. A noble and Godlike character is not a thing of favour or chance, but is the natural result of continued effort in right thinking, the effect of long-cherished association with Godlike thoughts. An ignoble and bestial character, by the same process, is the result of the continued harbouring of grovelling thoughts.

Man is made or unmade by himself; in the armoury of thought he forges the weapons by which he destroys himself; he also fashions the tools with which he builds for himself heavenly mansions of joy and strength and peace. By the right choice and true application of thought, man ascends to the Divine Perfection; by the abuse and wrong application of thought, he descends below the level of the beast. Between these two extremes are all the grades of character, and man is their maker and master.

Of all the beautiful truths pertaining to the soul which have been restored and brought to light in this age, none is more gladdening or fruitful of divine promise and confidence than this—that man is the master of thought, the moulder of character, and the maker and shaper of condition, environment, and destiny.

As a being of Power, Intelligence, and Love, and the lord of his own thoughts, man holds the key to every situation, and contains within himself that transforming and regenerative agency by which he may make himself what he wills.

Man is always the master, even in his weaker and most abandoned state; but in his weakness and degradation he is the foolish master who misgoverns his "household." When he begins to reflect upon his condition, and to search diligently for the Law upon which his being is established, he then becomes the wise master, directing his energies with intelligence, and fashioning his thoughts to fruitful issues. Such is the *conscious* master, and man can only thus become by discovering *within himself* the laws of thought; which discovery is totally a matter of application, self analysis, and experience.

Only by much searching and mining, are gold and diamonds obtained, and man can find every truth connected with his being, if he will dig deep into the mine of his soul; and that he is the maker of his character, the moulder of his life, and the builder of his destiny, he may unerringly prove, if he will watch, control, and alter his thoughts, tracing their effects upon himself, upon others, and upon his life and circumstances, linking cause and effect by patient practice and investigation, and utilizing his every experience, even to the most trivial, everyday occurrence, as a means of obtaining that knowledge of himself which is Understanding, Wisdom, Power. In this direction, as in no other, is the law absolute that "He that seeketh findeth; and to him that knocketh it shall be opened;" for only by patience, practice, and ceaseless importunity can a man enter the Door of the Temple of Knowledge.

EFFECT OF THOUGHT ON CIRCUMSTANCES

MAN'S mind may be likened to a garden, which may be intelligently cultivated or allowed to run wild; but whether cultivated or neglected, it must, and will, *bring forth*. If no useful seeds are *put* into it, then an abundance of useless weed-seeds will *fall* therein, and will continue to produce their kind.

Just as a gardener cultivates his plot, keeping it free from weeds, and growing the flowers and fruits which he requires, so may a man tend the garden of his mind, weeding out all the wrong, useless, and impure thoughts, and cultivating toward perfection the flowers and fruits of right, useful, and pure thoughts. By pursuing this process, a man sooner or later discovers that he is the master-gardener of his soul, the director of his life. He also reveals, within himself, the laws of thought, and understands, with ever-increasing accuracy, how the thought-forces and mind elements operate in the shaping of his character, circumstances, and destiny.

Thought and character are one, and as character can only manifest and discover itself through environment and circumstance, the outer conditions of a person's life will always be found to be harmoniously related to his inner state. This does not mean that a man's circumstances at any given time are an indication of his *entire* character, but that those circumstances are so intimately connected with some vital thought-element within himself that, for the time being, they are indispensable to his development.

Every man is where he is by the law of his being; the thoughts which he has built into his character have brought him there, and in the arrangement of his life there is no element of chance, but all is the result of a law which cannot err. This is just as true of those who feel "out of harmony" with their surroundings as of those who are contented with them.

As a progressive and evolving being, man is where he is that he may learn that he may grow; and as he learns the spiritual lesson which any circumstance contains for him, it passes away and gives place to other circumstances.

Man is buffeted by circumstances so long as he believes himself to be the creature of outside conditions, but when he realizes that he is a creative power, and that he may command the hidden soil and seeds of his being out of which circumstances grow, he then becomes the rightful master of himself.

That circumstances grow out of thought every man knows who has for any length of time practised self-control and self-purification, for he will have noticed that the alteration in his circumstances has been in exact ratio with his altered mental condition. So true is this that when a man earnestly applies himself to remedy the defects in his character, and makes swift and marked progress, he passes rapidly through a succession of vicissitudes.

The soul attracts that which it secretly harbours; that which it loves, and also that which it fears; it reaches the height of its cherished aspirations; it falls to the level of its unchastened desires,—and circumstances are the means by which the soul receives its own.

Every thought-seed sown or allowed to fall into the mind, and to take root there, produces its own, blossoming sooner or later into act, and bearing its own fruitage of opportunity and circumstance. Good thoughts bear good fruit, bad thoughts bad fruit.

The outer world of circumstance shapes itself to the inner world of thought, and both pleasant and unpleasant external conditions are factors, which make for the ultimate good of the individual. As the reaper of his own harvest, man learns both by suffering and bliss.

Following the inmost desires, aspirations, thoughts, by which he allows himself to be dominated, (pursuing the will-o'-the-wisps of impure imaginings or steadfastly walking the highway of strong and high endeavour), a man at last arrives at their fruition and fulfilment in the outer conditions of his life. The laws of growth and adjustment everywhere obtains.

A man does not come to the almshouse or the jail by the tyranny of fate or circumstance, but by the pathway of grovelling thoughts and base desires. Nor does a pure-minded man fall suddenly into crime by stress of any mere external force; the criminal thought had long been secretly fostered in the heart, and the hour of opportunity revealed its gathered power. Circumstance does not make the man; it reveals him to himself No such conditions can exist as descending into vice and its attendant sufferings apart from vicious inclinations, or ascending into virtue and its pure happiness without the continued cultivation of virtuous aspirations; and man, therefore, as the lord and master of thought, is the maker of himself the shaper and author of environment. Even at birth the soul comes to its own and through every step of its earthly pilgrimage it attracts those combinations of conditions which reveal itself, which are the reflections of its own purity and, impurity, its strength and weakness.

Men do not attract that which they *want*, but that which they *are*. Their whims, fancies, and ambitions are thwarted at every step, but their inmost thoughts and desires are fed with their own food, be it foul or clean. The "divinity that shapes our ends" is in ourselves; it is our very self. Only himself manacles man: thought and action are the gaolers of Fate—they imprison, being base; they are also the angels of Freedom—they liberate, being noble. Not what he wishes and prays for does a man get, but what he justly earns. His wishes and prayers are only gratified and answered when they harmonize with his thoughts and actions.

In the light of this truth, what, then, is the meaning of "fighting against circumstances?" It means that a man is continually revolting against an *effect* without, while all the time he is nourishing and preserving its *cause* in his heart. That cause may take the form of a conscious vice or an unconscious weakness; but whatever it is, it stubbornly retards the efforts of its possessor, and thus calls aloud for remedy.

Men are anxious to improve their circumstances, but are unwilling to improve themselves; they therefore remain bound. The man who does not shrink from self-crucifixion can never fail to accomplish the object upon which his heart is set. This is as true of earthly as of heavenly things. Even the man whose sole object is to acquire wealth must be prepared to make great personal sacrifices before he can accomplish his object; and how much more so he who would realize a strong and well-poised life?

Here is a man who is wretchedly poor. He is extremely anxious that his surroundings and home comforts should be improved, yet all the time he shirks his work, and considers he is justified in trying to deceive his employer on the ground of the insufficiency of his wages. Such a man does not understand the simplest rudiments of those principles which are the basis of true prosperity, and is not only totally unfitted to rise out of his wretchedness, but is actually attracting to himself a still deeper wretchedness by dwelling in, and acting out, indolent, deceptive, and unmanly thoughts.

Here is a rich man who is the victim of a painful and persistent disease as the result of gluttony. He is willing to give large sums of money to get rid of it, but he will not sacrifice his gluttonous desires. He wants to gratify his taste for rich and unnatural viands and have his health as well. Such a man is totally unfit to have health, because he has not yet learned the first principles of a healthy life.

Here is an employer of labour who adopts crooked measures to avoid paying the regulation wage, and, in the hope of making larger profits, reduces the wages of his workpeople. Such a man is altogether unfitted for prosperity, and when he finds himself bankrupt, both as regards reputation and riches, he blames circumstances, not knowing that he is the sole author of his condition.

I have introduced these three cases merely as illustrative of the truth that man is the causer (though nearly always is unconsciously) of his circumstances, and that, whilst aiming at a good end, he is continually frustrating its accomplishment by encouraging thoughts and desires which cannot possibly harmonize with that end. Such cases could be multiplied and varied almost indefinitely, but this is not necessary, as the reader can, if he so resolves, trace the action of the laws of thought in his own mind and life, and until this is done, mere external facts cannot serve as a ground of reasoning.

Circumstances, however, are so complicated, thought is so deeply rooted, and the conditions of happiness vary so, vastly with individuals, that a man's entire soul-condition (although it may be known to himself) cannot be judged by another from the external aspect of his life alone. A man may be honest in certain directions, yet suffer privations; a man may be dishonest in certain directions, yet acquire wealth; but the conclusion usually formed that the one man fails *because of his particular honesty*, and that the other *prospers because of his particular dishonesty*, is the result of a superficial judgment, which assumes that the dishonest man is almost totally corrupt, and the honest man almost entirely virtuous. In the light of a deeper knowledge and wider experience such judgment is found to be erroneous. The dishonest man may have some admirable virtues, which the other does, not possess; and the honest man obnoxious vices which are absent in the other. The honest man reaps the good results of his honest thoughts and acts; he also brings upon himself the sufferings, which his vices produce. The dishonest man likewise garners his own suffering and happiness.

It is pleasing to human vanity to believe that one suffers because of one's virtue; but not until a man has extirpated every sickly, bitter, and impure thought from his mind, and washed every sinful stain from his soul, can he be in a position to know and declare that his sufferings are the result of his good, and not of his bad qualities; and on the way to, yet long before he has reached, that supreme perfection, he will have found, working in his mind and life, the Great Law which is absolutely just, and which cannot, therefore, give good for evil, evil for good. Possessed of such knowledge, he will then know, looking back upon his past ignorance and blindness, that his life is, and always was, justly ordered, and that all his past experiences, good and bad, were the equitable outworking of his evolving, yet unevolved self.

Good thoughts and actions can never produce bad results; bad thoughts and actions can never produce good results. This is but saying that nothing can come from corn but corn, nothing from nettles but nettles. Men understand this law in the natural world, and work with it; but few understand it in the mental and moral world (though its operation there is just as simple and undeviating), and they, therefore, do not co-operate with it.

Suffering is *always* the effect of wrong thought in some direction. It is an indication that the individual is out of harmony with himself, with the Law of his being. The sole and supreme use of suffering is to purify, to burn out all that is useless and impure. Suffering ceases for him who is pure. There could be no object in burning gold after the dross had been removed, and a perfectly pure and enlightened being could not suffer.

The circumstances, which a man encounters with suffering, are the result of his own mental in harmony. The circumstances, which a man encounters with blessedness, are the result of his own mental harmony. Blessedness, not material possessions, is the measure of right thought; wretchedness, not lack of material possessions, is the measure of wrong thought. A man may be cursed and rich; he may be blessed and poor. Blessedness and riches are only joined together when the riches are rightly and wisely used; and the poor man only descends into wretchedness when he regards his lot as a burden unjustly imposed.

Indigence and indulgence are the two extremes of wretchedness. They are both equally unnatural and the result of mental disorder. A man is not rightly conditioned until he is a happy, healthy, and prosperous being; and happiness, health, and prosperity are the result of a harmonious adjustment of the inner with the outer, of the man with his surroundings.

A man only begins to be a man when he ceases to whine and revile, and commences to search for the hidden justice which regulates his life. And as he adapts his mind to that regulating factor, he ceases to accuse others as the cause of his condition, and builds himself up in strong and noble thoughts; ceases to kick against circumstances, but begins to *use* them as aids to his more rapid progress, and as a means of discovering the hidden powers and possibilities within himself.

Law, not confusion, is the dominating principle in the universe; justice, not injustice, is the soul and substance of life; and righteousness, not corruption, is the moulding and moving force in the spiritual government of the world. This being so, man has but to right himself to find that the universe is right; and during the process of putting himself right he will find that as he alters his thoughts towards things and other people, things and other people will alter towards him.

The proof of this truth is in every person, and it therefore admits of easy investigation by systematic introspection and self-analysis. Let a man radically alter his thoughts, and he will be astonished at the rapid transformation it will effect in the material conditions of his life. Men imagine that thought can be kept secret, but it cannot; it rapidly crystallizes into habit, and habit solidifies into circumstance. Bestial thoughts crystallize into habits of drunkenness and sensuality, which solidify into circumstances of destitution and disease: impure thoughts of every kind crystallize into enervating and confusing habits, which solidify into distracting and adverse circumstances: thoughts of fear, doubt, and indecision crystallize into weak, unmanly, and irresolute habits, which solidify into circumstances of failure, indigence, and slavish dependence: lazy thoughts crystallize into habits of uncleanliness and dishonesty, which solidify into circumstances of foulness and beggary: hateful and condemnatory thoughts crystallize into habits of accusation and violence, which solidify into circumstances of injury and persecution: selfish thoughts of all kinds crystallize into habits of self-seeking, which solidify into circumstances more or less distressing. On the other hand, beautiful thoughts of all kinds crystallize into habits of grace and kindliness, which solidify into genial and sunny circumstances: pure thoughts crystallize into habits of temperance and self-control, which solidify into circumstances of repose and peace: thoughts of courage, self-reliance, and decision crystallize into manly habits, which solidify into circumstances of success, plenty, and freedom: energetic thoughts crystallize into habits of cleanliness and industry, which solidify into circumstances of pleasantness: gentle and forgiving thoughts crystallize into habits of gentleness, which solidify into protective and preservative circumstances: loving and unselfish thoughts crystallize into habits of self-forgetfulness for others, which solidify into circumstances of sure and abiding prosperity and true riches.

A particular train of thought persisted in, be it good or bad, cannot fail to produce its results on the character and circumstances. A man cannot *directly* choose his circumstances, but he can choose his thoughts, and so indirectly, yet surely, shape his circumstances.

Nature helps every man to the gratification of the thoughts, which he most encourages, and opportunities are presented which will most speedily bring to the surface both the good and evil thoughts.

Let a man cease from his sinful thoughts, and all the world will soften towards him, and be ready to help him; let him put away his weakly and sickly thoughts, and lo, opportunities will spring up on every hand to aid his strong resolves; let him encourage good thoughts, and no hard fate shall bind him down to wretchedness and shame. The world is your kaleidoscope, and the varying combinations of colours, which at every succeeding moment it presents to you are the exquisitely adjusted pictures of your ever-moving thoughts.

"So You will be what you will to be;
Let failure find its false content
In that poor word, 'environment,'
But spirit scorns it, and is free.

"It masters time, it conquers space;
It cowes that boastful trickster, Chance,
And bids the tyrant Circumstance
Uncrown, and fill a servant's place.

"The human Will, that force unseen,
The offspring of a deathless Soul,
Can hew a way to any goal,
Though walls of granite intervene.
"Be not impatient in delays
But wait as one who understands;
When spirit rises and commands
The gods are ready to obey."

EFFECT OF THOUGHT ON HEALTH AND THE BODY

THE body is the servant of the mind. It obeys the operations of the mind, whether they be deliberately chosen or automatically expressed. At the bidding of unlawful thoughts the body sinks rapidly into disease and decay; at the command of glad and beautiful thoughts it becomes clothed with youthfulness and beauty.

Disease and health, like circumstances, are rooted in thought. Sickly thoughts will express themselves through a sickly body. Thoughts of fear have been known to kill a man as speedily as a bullet, and they are continually killing thousands of people just as surely though less rapidly. The people who live in fear of disease are the people who get it. Anxiety quickly demoralizes the whole body, and lays it open to the, entrance of disease; while impure thoughts, even if not physically indulged, will soon shatter the nervous system.

Strong, pure, and happy thoughts build up the body in vigour and grace. The body is a delicate and plastic instrument, which responds readily to the thoughts by which it is impressed, and habits of thought will produce their own effects, good or bad, upon it.

Men will continue to have impure and poisoned blood, so long as they propagate unclean thoughts. Out of a clean heart comes a clean life and a clean body. Out of a defiled mind proceeds a defiled life and a corrupt body. Thought is the fount of action, life, and manifestation; make the fountain pure, and all will be pure.

Change of diet will not help a man who will not change his thoughts. When a man makes his thoughts pure, he no longer desires impure food.

Clean thoughts make clean habits. The so-called saint who does not wash his body is not a saint. He who has strengthened and purified his thoughts does not need to consider the malevolent microbe.

If you would protect your body, guard your mind. If you would renew your body, beautify your mind. Thoughts of malice, envy, disappointment, despondency, rob the body of its health and grace. A sour face does not come by chance; it is made by sour thoughts. Wrinkles that mar are drawn by folly, passion, and pride.

I know a woman of ninety-six who has the bright, innocent face of a girl. I know a man well under middle age whose face is drawn into inharmonious contours. The one is the result of a sweet and sunny disposition; the other is the outcome of passion and discontent.

As you cannot have a sweet and wholesome abode unless you admit the air and sunshine freely into your rooms, so a strong body and a bright, happy, or serene countenance can only result from the free admittance into the mind of thoughts of joy and goodwill and serenity.

On the faces of the aged there are wrinkles made by sympathy, others by strong and pure thought, and others are carved by passion: who cannot distinguish them? With those who have lived righteously, age is calm, peaceful, and softly mellowed, like the setting sun. I have recently seen a philosopher on his deathbed. He was not old except in years. He died as sweetly and peacefully as he had lived.

There is no physician like cheerful thought for dissipating the ills of the body; there is no comforter to compare with goodwill for dispersing the shadows of grief and sorrow. To live continually in thoughts of ill will, cynicism, suspicion, and envy, is to be confined in a self made prison-hole. But to think well of all, to be cheerful with all, to patiently learn to find the good in all—such unselfish thoughts are the very portals of heaven; and to dwell day by day in thoughts of peace toward every creature will bring abounding peace to their possessor.

THOUGHT AND PURPOSE

Until thought is linked with purpose there is no intelligent accomplishment. With the majority the bark of thought is allowed to "drift" upon the ocean of life. Aimlessness is a vice, and such drifting must not continue for him who would steer clear of catastrophe and destruction.

They who have no central purpose in their life fall an easy prey to petty worries, fears, troubles, and self-pityings, all of which are indications of weakness, which lead, just as surely as deliberately planned sins (though by a different route), to failure, unhappiness, and loss, for weakness cannot persist in a power evolving universe.

A man should conceive of a legitimate purpose in his heart, and set out to accomplish it. He should make this purpose the centralizing point of his thoughts. It may take the form of a spiritual ideal, or it may be a worldly object, according to his nature at the time being; but whichever it is, he should steadily focus his thought-forces upon the object, which he has set before him. He should make this purpose his supreme duty, and should devote himself to its attainment, not allowing his thoughts to wander away into ephemeral fancies, longings, and imaginings. This is the royal road to self-control and true concentration of thought. Even if he fails again and again to accomplish his purpose (as he necessarily must until weakness is overcome), the *strength of character gained* will be the measure of *his true* success, and this will form a new starting-point for future power and triumph.

Those who are not prepared for the apprehension of a *great* purpose should fix the thoughts upon the faultless performance of their duty, no matter how insignificant their task may appear. Only in this way can the thoughts be gathered and focussed, and resolution and energy be developed, which being done, there is nothing which may not be accomplished.

The weakest soul, knowing its own weakness, and believing this truth *that strength can only be developed by effort and practice*, will, thus believing, at once begin to exert itself, and, adding effort to effort, patience to patience, and strength to strength, will never cease to develop, and will at last grow divinely strong.

As the physically weak man can make himself strong by careful and patient training, so the man of weak thoughts can make them strong by exercising himself in right thinking.

To put away aimlessness and weakness, and to begin to think with purpose, is to enter the ranks of those strong ones who only recognize failure as one of the pathways to attainment; who make all conditions serve them, and who think strongly, attempt fearlessly, and accomplish masterfully.

Having conceived of his purpose, a man should mentally mark out a *straight* pathway to its achievement, looking neither to the right nor the left. Doubts and fears should be rigorously excluded; they are disintegrating elements, which break up the straight line of effort, rendering it crooked, ineffectual, useless. Thoughts of doubt and fear never accomplished anything, and never can. They always lead to failure. Purpose, energy, power to do, and all strong thoughts cease when doubt and fear creep in.

The will to do springs from the knowledge that we *can* do. Doubt and fear are the great enemies of knowledge, and he who encourages them, who does not slay them. thwarts himself at every step.

He who has conquered doubt and fear has conquered failure. His every, thought is allied with power, and all difficulties are bravely met and wisely overcome. His purposes are seasonably planted, and they bloom and bring forth fruit, which does not fall prematurely to the ground.

Thought allied fearlessly to purpose becomes creative force: he who *knows* this is ready to become something higher and stronger than a mere bundle of wavering thoughts and fluctuating sensations; he who *does* this has become the conscious and intelligent wielder of his mental powers.

THE THOUGHT-FACTOR IN ACHIEVEMENT

ALL that a man achieves and all that he fails to achieve is the direct result of his own thoughts. In a justly ordered universe, where loss of equipoise would mean total destruction, individual responsibility must be absolute. A man's weakness and strength, purity and impurity, are his own, and not another man's; they are brought about by himself, and not by another; and they can only be altered by himself, never by another. His condition is also his own, and not another man's. His suffering and his happiness are evolved from within. As he thinks, so he is; as he continues to think, so he remains.

A strong man cannot help a weaker unless that weaker is *willing* to be helped, and even then the weak man must become strong of himself; he must, by his own efforts, develop the strength which he admires in another. None but himself can alter his condition.

It has been usual for men to think and to say, "Many men are slaves because one is an oppressor; let us hate the oppressor." Now, however, there is amongst an increasing few a tendency to reverse this judgment, and to say, "One man is an oppressor because many are slaves; let us despise the slaves."

The truth is that oppressor and slave are co-operators in ignorance, and, while seeming to afflict each other, are in reality afflicting themselves. A perfect Knowledge perceives the action of law in the weakness of the oppressed and the misapplied power of the oppressor; a perfect Love, seeing the suffering, which both states entail, condemns neither; a perfect Compassion embraces both oppressor and oppressed.

He who has conquered weakness, and has put away all selfish thoughts, belongs neither to oppressor nor oppressed. He is free.

A man can only rise, conquer, and achieve by lifting up his thoughts. He can only remain weak, and abject, and miserable by refusing to lift up his thoughts.

Before a man can achieve anything, even in worldly things, he must lift his thoughts above slavish animal indulgence. He may not, in order to succeed, give up all animality and selfishness, by any means; but a portion of it must, at least, be sacrificed. A man whose first thought is bestial indulgence could neither think clearly nor plan methodically; he could not find and develop his latent resources, and would fail in any undertaking. Not having commenced to manfully control his thoughts, he is not in a position to control affairs and to adopt serious responsibilities. He is not fit to act independently and stand alone. But he is limited only by the thoughts, which he chooses.

There can be no progress, no achievement without sacrifice, and a man's worldly success will be in the measure that he sacrifices his confused animal thoughts, and fixes his mind on the development of his plans, and the strengthening of his resolution and self-reliance. And the higher he lifts his thoughts, the more manly, upright, and righteous he becomes, the greater will be his success, the more blessed and enduring will be his achievements.

The universe does not favour the greedy, the dishonest, the vicious, although on the mere surface it may sometimes appear to do so; it helps the honest, the magnanimous, the virtuous. All the great Teachers of the ages have declared this in varying forms, and to prove and know it a man has but to persist in making himself more and more virtuous by lifting up his thoughts.

Intellectual achievements are the result of thought consecrated to the search for knowledge, or for the beautiful and true in life and nature. Such achievements may be sometimes connected with vanity and ambition, but they are not the outcome of those characteristics; they are the natural outgrowth of long and arduous effort, and of pure and unselfish thoughts.

Spiritual achievements are the consummation of holy aspirations. He who lives constantly in the conception of noble and lofty thoughts, who dwells upon all that is pure and unselfish, will, as surely as the sun reaches its zenith and the moon its full, become wise and noble in character, and rise into a position of influence and blessedness.

Achievement, of whatever kind, is the crown of effort, the diadem of thought. By the aid of self-control, resolution, purity, righteousness, and well-directed thought a man ascends; by the aid of animality, indolence, impurity, corruption, and confusion of thought a man descends.

A man may rise to high success in the world, and even to lofty altitudes in the spiritual realm, and again descend into weakness and wretchedness by allowing arrogant, selfish, and corrupt thoughts to take possession of him.

Victories attained by right thought can only be maintained by watchfulness. Many give way when success is assured, and rapidly fall back into failure.

All achievements, whether in the business, intellectual, or spiritual world, are the result of definitely directed thought, are governed by the same law and are of the same method; the only difference lies in *the object of attainment*.

He who would accomplish little must sacrifice little; he who would achieve much must sacrifice much; he who would attain highly must sacrifice greatly.

VISIONS AND IDEALS

THE dreamers are the saviours of the world. As the visible world is sustained by the invisible, so men, through all their trials and sins and sordid vocations, are nourished by the beautiful visions of their solitary dreamers. Humanity cannot forget its dreamers; it cannot let their ideals fade and die; it lives in them; it knows them as they *realities* which it shall one day see and know.

Composer, sculptor, painter, poet, prophet, sage, these are the makers of the after-world, the architects of heaven. The world is beautiful because they have lived; without them, labouring humanity would perish.

He who cherishes a beautiful vision, a lofty ideal in his heart, will one day realize it. Columbus cherished a vision of another world, and he discovered it; Copernicus fostered the vision of a multiplicity of worlds and a wider universe, and he revealed it; Buddha beheld the vision of a spiritual world of stainless beauty and perfect peace, and he entered into it.

Cherish your visions; cherish your ideals; cherish the music that stirs in your heart, the beauty that forms in your mind, the loveliness that drapes your purest thoughts, for out of them will grow all delightful conditions, all, heavenly environment; of these, if you but remain true to them, your world will at last be built.

To desire is to obtain; to aspire is to, achieve. Shall man's basest desires receive the fullest measure of gratification, and his purest aspirations starve for lack of sustenance? Such is not the Law: such a condition of things can never obtain: "ask and receive."

Dream lofty dreams, and as you dream, so shall you become. Your Vision is the promise of what you shall one day be; your Ideal is the prophecy of what you shall at last unveil.

The greatest achievement was at first and for a time a dream. The oak sleeps in the acorn; the bird waits in the egg; and in the highest vision of the soul a waking angel stirs. Dreams are the seedlings of realities.

Your circumstances may be uncongenial, but they shall not long remain so if you but perceive an Ideal and strive to reach it. You cannot travel *within* and stand still *without*. Here is a youth hard pressed by poverty and labour; confined long hours in an unhealthy workshop; unschooled, and lacking all the arts of refinement. But he dreams of better things; he thinks of intelligence, of refinement, of grace and beauty. He conceives of, mentally builds up, an ideal condition of life; the vision of a wider liberty and a larger scope takes possession of him; unrest urges him to action, and he utilizes all his spare time and means, small though they are, to the development of his latent powers and resources. Very soon so altered has his mind become that the workshop can no longer hold him. It has become so out of harmony with his mentality that it falls out of his life as a garment is cast aside, and, with the growth of opportunities, which fit the scope of his expanding powers, he passes out of it forever. Years later we see this youth as a full-grown man. We find him a master of certain forces of the mind, which he wields with worldwide influence and almost unequalled power. In his hands he holds the cords of gigantic responsibilities; he speaks, and lo, lives are changed; men and women hang upon his words and remould their characters, and, sunlike, he becomes the fixed and luminous centre round which innumerable destinies revolve. He has realized the Vision of his youth. He has become one with his Ideal.

And you, too, youthful reader, will realize the Vision (not the idle wish) of your heart, be it base or beautiful, or a mixture of both, for you will always gravitate toward that which you, secretly, most love. Into your hands will be placed the exact results of your own thoughts; you will receive that which you earn; no more, no less. Whatever your present environment may be, you will fall, remain, or rise with your thoughts, your Vision, your Ideal. You will become as small as your controlling desire; as great as your dominant aspiration: in the beautiful words of Stanton Kirkham Davis, "You may be keeping accounts, and presently you shall walk out of the door that for so long has seemed to you the barrier of your ideals, and shall find yourself before an audience—the pen still behind your ear, the ink stains on your fingers and then and there shall pour out the torrent of your inspiration. You may be driving sheep, and you shall wander to the city-bucolic and open-mouthed; shall wander under the intrepid guidance of the spirit into the studio of the master, and after a time he shall say, 'I have nothing more to teach you.' And now you have become the master, who did so recently dream of great things while driving sheep. You shall lay down the saw and the plane to take upon yourself the regeneration of the world."

The thoughtless, the ignorant, and the indolent, seeing only the apparent effects of things and not the things themselves, talk of luck, of fortune, and chance. Seeing a man grow rich, they say, "How lucky he is!" Observing another become intellectual, they exclaim, "How highly favoured he is!" And noting the saintly character and wide influence of another, they remark, "How chance aids him at every turn!" They do not see the trials and failures and struggles which these men have voluntarily encountered in order to gain their experience; have no knowledge of the sacrifices they have made, of the undaunted efforts they have put forth, of the faith they have exercised, that they might overcome the apparently insurmountable, and realize the Vision of their heart. They do not know the darkness and the heartaches; they only see the light and joy, and call it "luck". They do not see the long and arduous journey, but only behold the pleasant goal, and call it "good fortune," do not understand the process, but only perceive the result, and call it chance.

In all human affairs there are *efforts*, and there are *results*, and the strength of the effort is the measure of the result. Chance is not. Gifts, powers, material, intellectual, and spiritual possessions are the fruits of effort; they are thoughts completed, objects accomplished, visions realized.

The Vision that you glorify in your mind, the Ideal that you enthrone in your heart—this you will build your life by, this you will become.

SERENITY

CALMNESS of mind is one of the beautiful jewels of wisdom. It is the result of long and patient effort in self-control. Its presence is an indication of ripened experience, and of a more than ordinary knowledge of the laws and operations of thought.

A man becomes calm in the measure that he understands himself as a thought evolved being, for such knowledge necessitates the understanding of others as the result of thought, and as he develops a right understanding, and sees more and more clearly the internal relations of things by the action of cause and effect he ceases to fuss and fume and worry and grieve, and remains poised, steadfast, serene.

The calm man, having learned how to govern himself, knows how to adapt himself to others; and they, in turn, reverence his spiritual strength, and feel that they can learn of him and rely upon him. The more tranquil a man becomes, the greater is his success, his influence, his power for good. Even the ordinary trader will find his business prosperity increase as he develops a greater self-control and equanimity, for people will always prefer to deal with a man whose demeanour is strongly equable.

The strong, calm man is always loved and revered. He is like a shade-giving tree in a thirsty land, or a sheltering rock in a storm. "Who does not love a tranquil heart, a sweet-tempered, balanced life? It does not matter whether it rains or shines, or what changes come to those possessing these blessings, for they are always sweet, serene, and calm. That exquisite poise of character, which we call serenity is the last lesson of culture, the fruitage of the soul. It is precious as wisdom, more to be desired than gold—yea, than even fine gold. How insignificant mere money seeking looks in comparison with a serene life—a life that dwells in the ocean of Truth, beneath the waves, beyond the reach of tempests, in the Eternal Calm!

"How many people we know who sour their lives, who ruin all that is sweet and beautiful by explosive tempers, who destroy their poise of character, and make bad blood! It is a question whether the great majority of people do not ruin their lives and mar their happiness by lack of self-control. How few people we meet in life who are well balanced, who have that exquisite poise which is characteristic of the finished character!

Yes, humanity surges with uncontrolled passion, is tumultuous with ungoverned grief, is blown about by anxiety and doubt only the wise man, only he whose thoughts are controlled and purified, makes the winds and the storms of the soul obey him.

Tempest-tossed souls, wherever ye may be, under whatsoever conditions ye may live, know this in the ocean of life the isles of Blessedness are smiling, and the sunny shore of your ideal awaits your coming. Keep your hand firmly upon the helm of thought. In the bark of your soul reclines the commanding Master; He does but sleep: wake Him. Self-control is strength; Right Thought is mastery; Calmness is power. Say unto your heart, "Peace, be still!"

Thoughts are Things
by Prentice Mulford

Chapter 1: The Material Mind Versus The Spiritual Mind

There belongs to every human being a higher self and a lower self--a self or mind of the spirit which has been growing for ages, and a self of the body, which is but a thing of yesterday. The higher self is full of prompting idea, suggestion and aspiration. This it receives of the Supreme Power. All this the lower or animal self regards as wild and visionary. The higher self argues possibilities and power for us greater than men and women now possess and enjoy. The lower self says we can only live and exist as men and women have lived and existed before us. The higher self craves freedom from the cumbrousness, the limitations, the pains and disabilities of the body. The lower self says that we are born to them, born to ill, born to suffer, and must suffer as have so many before us. The higher self wants a standard for right and wrong of its own. The lower self says we must accept a standard made for us by others--by general and long-held opinion, belief and prejudice.

"To thine own self be true" is an oft-uttered adage. But to which self? The higher or lower?

You have in a sense two minds--the mind of the body and the mind of the spirit.

Spirit is a force and a mystery. All we know or may ever know of it is that it exists, and is ever working and producing all results in physical things seen of physical sense and many more not so seen.

What is seen, of any object, a tree, an animal, a stone, a man is only a part of that tree, animal, stone, or man. There is a force which for a time binds such objects together in the form you see them. That force is always acting on them to greater or lesser degree. It builds up the flower to its fullest maturity. Its cessation to act on the flower or tree causes what we call decay. It is constantly changing the shape of all forms of what are called organized matter. An animal, a plant, a human being are not in physical shape this month or this year what they will be next month or next year.

This ever-acting, ever-varying force, which lies behind and, in a sense, creates all forms of matter we call Spirit.

To see, reason and judge of life and things in the knowledge of this force makes what is termed the "Spiritual Mind."

We have through knowledge the wonderful power of using or directing this force, when we recognize it, and know that it exists so as to bring us health, happiness and eternal peace of mind. Composed as we are of this force, we are ever attracting more of it to us and making it a part of our being.

With more of this force must come more and more knowledge. At first in our physical existances we allow it to work blindly. Then we are in the ignorance of that condition known as the material mind. But as mind through its growth or increase of this power becomes more and more awakened, it asks: "Why comes so much of pain, grief and disappointment in the physical life?" "Why do we seem born to suffer and decay"

That question is the first awakening cry of the spiritual mind, and an earnest question or demand for knowledge must in time be answered.

The material mind is a part of yourself, which has been appropriated by the body and educated by the body. It is as if you taught a child that the wheels of a steamboat made the boat move, and said nothing of the steam, which gives the real power. Bred in such ignorance, the child, should the wheels stop moving, would look no farther for the cause of their stoppage than to try to find where to repair them, very much as now so many depend entirely on repair of the physical body to ensure its healthy, vigorous movement, never dreaming that the imperfection lies in the real motive power--the mind.

The mind of the body or material mind sees, thinks and judges entirely from the material or physical standpoint. It sees in your own body all there is of you. The spiritual mind sees the body as an instrument for the mind or real self to use in dealing with material things. The material mind sees in the death of the body an end of all there is of you. The spiritual mind sees in the death of the body only the falling off from the spirit of a worn-out instrument. It knows that you exist as before only invisible to the physical eye. The material mind sees your physical strength as coming entirely from your muscles and sinews, and not from source without your body.

It sees in such persuasive power, as you may have with tongue or pen, the only force you possess for dealing with people to accomplish results The spiritual mind will know in time that your thought influences people for or against your interests, though their bodies are thousands of miles distant. The material mind does not regard its thought as an actual element as real as air or water. The spiritual mind knows that every one of its thousand daily secret thoughts are real things acting on the minds of the persons they are sent to. The spiritual mind knows that matter or the material is only an expression of spirit or force; that such matter is ever changing in accordance with the spirit that makes or externalizes itself in the form we call matter, and therefore, if the thought of health, strength and recuperation is constantly held to in the mind, such thought of health, strength and rejuvenation will express itself in the body, making maturity never ceasing, vigour never ending, and the keenness of every physical sense ever increasing.

The material mind thinks matter, or that which is known by our physical senses, to be the largest part of what exists. The spiritual mind regards matter as the coarser or cruder expression of spirit and the smallest part of what really exists. The material mind is made sad at the contemplation of decay. The spiritual mind attaches little importance to decay, knowing in such decay that spirit or the moving force in all things is simply taking the dead body or the rotten tree to pieces, and that it will build them up again as before temporarily into some other new physical form of life and beauty. The mind of the body thinks that its physical senses of seeing, hearing and feeling constitute all the senses you possess. The higher mind or mind of the spirit knows that it possesses other senses akin to those of physical sight and hearing, but more powerful and far reaching.

The mind of the body has been variously termed "the material mind," the "mortal mind " and the "carnal mind." All these refer to the same mind, or, in other words to that part of your real sell which has been educated in error by the body.

If you had been born and bred entirely among people who believed that the earth was a flat surface and did not revolve around the sun, you would in the earlier years of your physical growth believe as they did. Exactly in such fashion do you in your earlier years absorb the thought and belief of those nearest you, who think that the body is all there is of them, and judge of everything by its physical interpretation to them. This makes your material mind.

The material mind seeing, what seems to it, depth, dissolution and decay in all human organization, and ignorant of the fact that the real self or intelligence has in such seeming death only cast off a worn-out envelope, thinks that decay and death is the ultimate of all humanity. For such reason it cannot avoid a gloom or sadness coming of such error, which now pervades so much of human life at present. One result or reaction from such gloom born of hopelessness is a reckless spirit for getting every possible gratification and pleasure, regardless of right and justice so long as the present body lasts. This is a great mistake. All pleasure so gained cannot be lasting. It brings besides a hundredfold more misery and disappointment.

The spiritual mind teaches that pleasure is the great aim of existence. But it points out ways and means for gaining lasting happiness other than those coming of the teaching of the material mind. The spiritual mind, or mind opened to higher and newer forces of life, teaches that there is a law regulating the exercise of every physical sense. When we learn and follow this law, our gratifications and possessions do not prove sources of greater pain than happiness, as they do to so many.

By the spiritual mind is meant a clearer mental sight of things and forces existing both in us and the Universe, and of which the race for the most part has been in total ignorance. We have now but a glimpse of these forces, those of some being relatively a little clearer than those of others. But enough has been shown to convince a few that the real and existing causes for humanity's sickness, sorrow and disappointment have not in the past been seen at all. In other words, the race has been as children, fancying that the miller inside was turning the arms of the windmill, because some person had so told them. So taught their would remain in total ignorance that the wind was the motive power.

This illustration is not at all an overdrawn picture of the existing ignorance which rejects the idea that thought is an element all about us as plentiful as air, and that as blindly directed by individuals and masses of individuals in the domain of material mind or ignorance, it is turning the windmill's arms, sometimes in one direction, sometimes in another; sometimes with good and sometimes with evil results.

A suit of clothes is not the body that wears such suit. Yet the material mind reasons very much in this way. It knows of no such thing as clothing for the spirit, for it does not know that body and spirit are two distinct things. It reasons that the suit of clothing (the body) is all there is of the man or woman. When that man or woman tumbles to pieces through weakness, it sees only the suit of clothes so going to pieces, and all its efforts to make that man or woman stronger are put on the suit instead of making effort to reinforce the power within which has made the suit.

There are probably no two individuals precisely alike as regards the relative condition or action on them of their material and spiritual minds. With some the spiritual seems not at all awakened. With others it has begun to stretch and rub its eyes as a person does on physical awakening, when everything still appears vague and indistinct. Others are more fully awakened. They feel to greater or lesser extent that there are forces belonging to them before unthought of. It is with such that the struggle for mastery between the material and spiritual mind is likely to be most severe, and such struggle for a time is likely to be accompanied by physical disturbance, pain or lack of ease.

The material mind is, until won over and convinced of the truths, constantly received by the spiritual mind at war and in opposition to it The ignorant part of yourself dislikes very much to give up its long accustomed habits of thinking. Its costs a struggle in any case at first to own that we have been mistaken and give up views long held to.

The material mind wants to more on in a rut of life and idea, as it always has done, and as thousands are now doing. It dislikes change more and more as the crust of the old thought held from year to year grows more thickly over it. It wants to live on and on in the house it has inhabited for years; dress in the fashion of the past; go to business and return year in and year out at precisely the same hour. It rejects and despises after a certain age the idea of learning any new accomplishments, such as painting or music, whose greatest use is to divert the mind, rest it, and enable you to live in other departments of being, all this being apart from the pleasure also given you as the mind or spirit teaches the body more and more skill and expertness in the art you pursue.

The material mind sees as the principal use of any art only a means to bring money, and not in such art a means for giving variety to life, dispelling weariness, resting that portion of the mind devoted to other business, improving health and increasing vigour of mind and body. It holds to the idea of being "too old to learn."

This is the condition of so many persons who have arrived at or are past " middle age." They want to "settle down." They accept as inevitable the idea of "growing old." Their material mind tells them that their bodies must gradually weaken, shrink from the fullness and proportion of youth, decay and finally die.

Material minds say this always has been, and therefore always must be. They accept the idea wholly. They say quite unconsciously, "It must be."

To say a thing must be, is the very power that makes it. The material mind then sees the body ever as gradually decaying, even though it dislikes the picture, and puts it out of sight as much as possible. But the idea will recur from time to time as suggested by the death of their contemporaries, and as it does they think " must," and that state of mind indicated by the word "must" will inevitably bring material results in decay.

The spiritual or more enlightened mind says: "If you would help to drive away sickness, turn your thought as much as you can on health, strength and vigour, and on strong, healthy, vigorous material things, such as moving clouds, fresh breezes, the cascade, the ocean surge; on woodland scenes and growing healthy trees; on birds full of life and motion; for in so doing you turn on yourself a real current or this healthy life-giving thought, which is suggested and brought you by the thought of such vigorous, strong material objects.

And above all, try to rely and trust that Supreme Power which formed all these things and far more and which is the endless and inexhaustible part of your higher self or spiritual mind, and as your faith increases in this Power, so will your own power ever increase.

Nonsense! " says the ultra material mind. " If my body is sick, I must have something done to cure that body with things I can see and feel, and that is the only thing to be done. As for thinking, it makes no difference what I think, sick or well."

At present in such a case a mind whose sense of these truths new to it, has just commenced to be awakened, will, in many cases, allow itself to be for a time overpowered and ridiculed out of such an idea by its own material mind or uneducated part of itself; and in this it is very likely to be assisted by other material minds, who have not woke up at all to these truths, and who are temporarily all the stronger through the positiveness of ignorance. These are as people who cannot see as far ahead as one may with a telescope, and who may be perfectly honest in their disbelief regarding what the person with the telescope does see. Though such people do not speak a word or argue against the belief of the partly awakened mind, still their thought acts on such a mind as a bar or blind to these glimpses of the truth.

But when the spiritual mind has once commenced to awaken, nothing can stop its further waking, though the material may for a time retard it.

"Your real self may not at times be where your body is" says the spiritual mind. It is where your mind is--in the store, the office, the workshop, or with some person to whom you are strongly attached, and all of these may be in towns or cities far from the one your body resides in. Your real self moves with inconceivable rapidity as your thought moves. "Nonsense" says your material mind; "I myself am wherever my body is, and nowhere else"

Many a thought or idea that you reject as visionary, or as a whim or fancy, comes of the prompting of your spiritual mind. It is your material mind that rejects it.

No such idea comes but that there is a truth in it. But that truth we may not be able to carry out to a relative perfection immediately. Two hundred years ago some mind may have seen the use of steam as a motive power. But that motive power could not then have been carried out as it is today. A certain previous growth was necessary--a growth and improvement in the manufacture of iron, in the construction of roads, and in the needs of the people.

But the idea was a truth. Held to by various minds, it has brought steam as a motive power to its present relative perfection. It has struggled against and overcome every argument and obstacle placed in its way by dull, material, plodding minds. When you entertain any idea and say to yourself in substance: "Well, such a thing may be, though I cannot now see it" you remove a great barrier to the carrying out and realization by yourself of the new and strange possibilities in store for you.

The spiritual mind today sees belonging to itself a power for accomplishing any and all results in the physical world, greater than the masses dream of. It sees that as regards life's possibilities we are still in dense ignorance. It sees however, a few things--namely, perfect health, freedom from decay, weakness and death of the body, power of transit, travel and observation independent of the body, and methods for obtaining all needful and desirable material things through the action and working of silent mind or thought, either singly or in co-operation with others.

The condition of mind to be desired is the entire dominancy of the spiritual mind. But this does not imply dominancy or control in any sense of tyrannical mastership of the material mind by the spiritual mind. It does imply that the material mind will be swept away so far as its stubborn resistance and opposition to the promptings of the spiritual are concerned. It implies that the body will become the willing servant, or rather assistant of the spirit. It implies that the material mind will not endeavour to act itself up as the superior when it is only the inferior. It implies that state when the body will gladly lend its co-operation to all the desires of the spiritual mind.

Then all power can be given your spirit. Then no force need be expended in resisting the hostility of the material mind. Then all such force will be used to further our undertakings, to bring us material goods, to raise us higher and higher into realms of power, peace and happiness, to accomplish what now would be called miracles.

Neither the material mind nor the material body is to be won over and merged into the spiritual by any course of severe self censure or self denial, nor self punishment in expiation for sins committed, nor asceticism. That will only make you the more harsh, severe, bigoted and merciless, both to yourself and others. It is out of this perversion of the truth that have arisen such terms as " crucifying the body" and " subjugating the lower or animal mind." It is from this perversion that have come orders and associations of men and women who, going to another extreme, seek holiness in self denial and penance.

"Holiness" implies wholeness, or whole action of the spirit on the body, or perfect control by your spirit over a body, through knowledge and faith in our capacity to draw ever more and more from the Supreme Power.

When you get out of patience with yourself, through the aggressiveness of the material mind, through your frequent slips and falls into your besetting sins through periods of petulance or ill temper, or excess in any direction, you do no good, and only ill in calling or thinking for yourself hard names. You should not call yourself "a vile sinner" anymore than you would call any other person a "vile sinner," If you do, you put out in thought the "vile sinner" and make it temporarily a reality. If in your mental vision you teach yourself that you are "utterly depraved" and a "vile sinner," you are unconsciously making that your ideal, and you will unconsciously grow up to it until the pain and evil coming of such unhealthy growth either makes you turn back or destroys your body, For out of this state of mind, which in the past has been much inculcated, comes harshness, bigotry, lack of charity for others, hard, stern and gloomy and unhealthy views of life, and these mental conditions will surely bring physical disease.

When the material mind is put away, or, in other words, then we become convinced of the existence of these spiritual forces, both in ourselves, and outside of ourselves, and when we learn to use them rightly (for we are now and always have been using them in some way), then to use the words of Paul: " Faith is swallowed up in victory," and the sting and fear of death is removed. Life becomes then one glorious advance forward from the pleasure of today to the greater pleasure of tomorrow, and the phrase "to live" means only to enjoy.

Chapter 2: Who Are Our Relations?

The man or woman who if most like you in tastes, motives, and habits of thought, and to whom you feel most attracted, may not be brother, sister, cousin, or any physical relative at all. But such person is to you a very near relation.

Your brothers or sisters may not be like you at all in mind, taste, and inclination. You may associate with them because they are members of the family, but were you not to know them as brothers, sisters, or other relatives, or were you to see elsewhere their exact counterparts in character, you might not like such counterparts at all.

Physical or " blood relationship" has very little bearing on the real or mental relationship. It is possible for a brother or sister, a father or mother to be very closely allied to you in thought and sympathy. Again, it is possible for a father or mother, brother or sister, to be very remote from you in thought and sympathy, and to live in a realm or atmosphere of thought very unlike yours.

You can live neither healthfully nor comfortably, unless with those whose thought-atmosphere (a literal emanation from them) is similar to your own. Physical relationship may or may not furnish such at atmosphere. Compel a labouring man whose thought goes little beyond his eating, drinking and daily round of work, to live exclusively with a company of artists and philosophers, seeing none of his own kind and order of thought, and that man's spirits would in time be depressed, and his health would suffer. The same law works when the superior mind is compelled to constant association with the inferior. Such may be your position among physical relatives.

Children live, thrive and are exhilarated by the thought-atmosphere emanating from their playmates. Cut them entirely off from such association and they droop. As a child, you lived upon this atmosphere of childhood; that is, you lived in the spiritual relationship of childhood, and regarding a certain playful thought nutriment, received it and also gave it to your playmates. You may wonder now why you cannot arouse the old feeling and exhilaration coming either from the associations of childhood or youth. It is because your spirit requires another thought food or atmosphere, which only another and probably higher order of mind can give. That received, and time would pass as quickly and pleasantly as it did with the associates of your earlier physical existence.

Those who can furnish it are your real relations. But such relationship cannot exist unless you can furnish them with the same quality of thought in return. The real or spiritual relations of many merchants, mechanics, and those of other callings, are their brother merchants, mechanics, or those of similar occupations. They prove this by their lives. They feel more at home with those whose business is like their own than they do in the places they may call home, to which they resort to eat, sleep, and spend often a tiresome Sunday, longing for Monday's coming, and the more welcome life of the market-stall and store. Because there they are amongst their real relations, and are being literally led and stimulated by the thought- atmosphere furnished them by these relatives, which they also furnish in turn.

Every order of mind or quality of thought must have association with a corresponding order of mind and quality of thought, or it will suffer. But "blood relationship" has little to do with furnishing such order of thought.

There is a vast amount of unconscious tyranny exercised through the ties of physical relationship. Children often, when grown up, place the mothers or fathers in their minds in a sphere and method of life where they may or may not care to belong. Then thought, seldom if ever expressed, runs in substance thus: "Mother is getting too old to wear bright colours. She must dress more subdued." " It is ridiculous for mother (if a widow) to marry again" (very hard cash reasons sometimes entering into this sentiment). " Mother, of course, does not want to enter into our gayer life, so she can stay at home and take care of the children." or, " It is time father retired from business," or, " Father's idea of marrying again is ridiculous."

No force is more subtle in its workings, nor more powerful to bring results for good or ill than the steady output of thought from one or several minds combined, on one person to effect some desired result, and whether this is done intelligently and consciously, or blindly, the force works the same result.

Now a continual flow of this kind of thought, coming from, possibly, three or four minds to whom "mother" was instrumental in furnishing new bodies, and continually directed on "mother," is a very powerful force to direct and keep her exactly where the children find it most convenient to have her. The whole conventional current of thought also flows as an aid in this direction. "Mother," says this unspoken sentiment, "must of course grow old, retire gradually from a more active and gayer life, and retire also to a corner of the household, to associate with other shelved and declining parents, and he useful as a general upper nurse in times of sickness or other family emergency." Through the action on her on these minds, many mothers cease to have any privileges as individuals, and eventually do exactly as their children desire.

Possibly it is here remarked or thought, "But should I not go to my mother or other near relative with my cares and trials, and receive her help, as I have always been in the habit of doing? Ought not those of my own family, above all others, to help me in time of need?"

Certainly, if the mother or any of your physical relatives are glad and anxious so to do. Certainly, if such service from a relative comes directly from the heart and is not impelled by the sentiment taking sometimes this form of unspoken expression: "I suppose I must do this because it is my brother, or my son, or other physical relative who asks it." Asks it? Many,

many are these services which are unconsciously demanded, rather than asked, in these cases. Loads are piled upon relatives simply because they are relatives. Favours in money--in the endorsement of notes, are in a sense exacted through sympathy of relatives. Support, food, shelter, maintenance, are expected from relatives when it cannot be procured elsewhere. Hospitality is expected from relatives, when to expect hospitality is to make such entertainment the result of a demand. Presents are expected from relatives, when to expect a gift makes it rather an extortion.

Real gifts are always surprises. No one expects a surprise since expectation destroys surprise. Relatives visit and "camp down" on other relatives simply because they are relatives, and a vast amount of grudging, grumbling, but unspoken thought is always going out when relatives use each other's houses to save hotel bills.

No real or lasting good comes of any gift bestowed on another unless the heart goes with it, and its bestowal is to the giver an act of unalloyed pleasure. Because something else goes with the material gift, the food, the shelter, the loan, which though not seen, and little known, is more important than the form itself. That is the thought which goes with it, That thought strongly affects, for good or ill, the person who receives the gift. If, as giving within your means, you bestow the merest trifle in money upon a person in need, and the thought that goes with it is not only the most sincere desire to help that person, but you feel a keen sense of pleasure in giving such help, then you throw upon that person a certain thought-element which will never leave them, and benefit them eternally and in proportion to the quality, power and force of your thought. Then you do far more than relieve their present physical necessity. You give them a certain amount of spiritual power. Your wish that their power may be so developed and increased as to enable them to live above beggary, and draw to themselves the goods of this earth (as all will and must, when grown to a certain stature in spiritual power), is a great help for them in time to acquire such power. You have sent and sown in them a seed of thought which will take root and bear fruit at some period of their real or spiritual existence.

But if you give grudgingly, if you give under any sort of compulsion, if you give food, shelter, clothing, money, anything, only because circumstances compel you so to do, or because people might talk unfavourably of you for not giving, or because other people are so giving, then your gift does relatively little good, no matter on whom bestowed, be it even mother, father, brother, sister, son or daughter.

You relieve, then, only a physical necessity, and that only for a time. You may possibly feed a body, shelter it, clothe it. But you do not, and cannot feed properly the spirit that uses that body if the thought going with your gift is not that of the most perfect willingness and hearty pleasure in relieving that body's necessities. The grudging thought accompanying the gift, the thought common to that position when the recipient of the gift (no matter how near the relationship) is endured rather than enjoyed, the thought accompanying any gift to any person, or relative, that is given principally because custom and public opinion require it, or because of the recipient's importunity, is a great damage both to giver and taker. It is the sending to the one who receives a current of thought, evil in its character and result. It brings back to the giver from the one who takes a response in thought of like nature, and this also is harmful. Because, if you receive a gift which you have in any way extorted your feeling for the giver is not that of warm, glowing gratitude, but something quite different.

The Christ of Judea, when commending the widow who cast her mite into the treasury, did so in our estimation and as seen in this light, not merely because she gave in proportion to her material means, but because he saw that her thought of desire to help in whatever way help was needed, going with that mite, was far more heartfelt and genuine than that of richer people who cast in larger sums, but cast in also with them a lower character of thought and motive. He saw, also, that the woman's thought was actually doing far more to help than that of the others, for it was purer, less mixed with lower motive and therefore far the stronger.

"Is it not my duty," some may ask, "to feed, clothe, shelter, and support a very near relative or parent, if helpless, in their old age?"

The term "doing from a sense of duty" does not always imply that the thing done, be it the person helped or the patient nursed through sickness, is done from the impulse of love for that person or love for the doing. It is sometimes done mechanically, or with dislike for the doing. It is sometimes a forced and painful performance. For such reason little good is done, for if physical necessities are temporarily relieved, spiritual necessities are not, and unless the spiritual portion of our natures is fed there can be no permanent relief or good done the physical. Parents who in old age are supported by their children merely from a sense of duty, have sometimes their spirits wounded and starved--wounded, because they feel they are endured encumbrances---starved, because no real love goes with the gift or service done by these children. Children who come into the world unwelcomed by the parent and are brought up only because custom, conventionality and public opinion demand their support from that parent, are most unfortunate, and suffer from the blight and starvation thereby caused their spirits. Genuine heartfelt love is literally life giving, and if received by the child is for it a source of cheer, health, strength, and activity.

There is a certain trained conscience whose basis of education is fear of public or private opinion. This sometimes really impels acts which are said to be done from a "sense of duty." If public opinion should suddenly change, and cast no censure at all on the person who refused to support very near relatives in want or old age, a proportion of such relatives would probably go to the poor-house, and the son or daughter who sent them there would be acting out their real natures, and not feigning a sentiment they did not possess.

Mothers sometimes say, "I don't care what becomes of me, so that my children are well brought up and educated." A mother should care a great deal for her own cultivation. If her cultivation and growth in wisdom are checked, that of her children will be checked. It will be checked if she sinks herself in her endeavour to favour her children. A genuine mother will continually compel the admiration and respect, as well as love of her children. Such admiration and respect can be compelled only by a woman who knows the world, has standing and position in it and is ever pushing forward to more commanding place and position. Such admiration and respect from son or daughter cannot be compelled by the mother who retires to a household corner, becomes a cross between upper nurse and governess, neglects her dress and personal appearance, and teaches her children that she is at their disposal and use in all family emergencies, real or fancied. For this very reason are many mothers ignored, snubbed, and ridiculed by their grown-up children.

If mothers so sink themselves, as they falsely imagine, to benefit their children, they pay in cases a terrible penalty. If you allow your will constantly to be overborne by another; if you give up your own preferences and inclinations, and become only another's echo; if you live just as others desire, you will lose more and more, for this existence, the power of self-assertion; you will absorb so much of the other mind and thought about you as to become a part of that mind, and so act in accordance even with its silent will and unspoken desire; you will fossilize, and sink into a hopeless servitude; you will lose more and more of both physical and mental power for doing anything; you will become the chimney-corner encumbrance, the senile parent, the helpless old man or woman, endured rather than loved.

This, in many instances, has been the effect of the grown-up children's minds upon a parent. It is the silent force of those minds, continually working on that of the parent, which helps to break the parent down physically, and the decay and mental weakness, commonly charged to "advancing years," is due in part to the injurious effect of a mind or group of minds, seeking to usurp and overpower another. This evil is done unconsciously. The son wishes to manage the farm. His will may be strong. He gains power step by step. He takes as rights what at first he took only by a father's permission or as privileges. He goes on step by step, having his way in all things, great and small, perhaps being aided by others of the children, using their silent force in the same direction. And this may be a combined force almost impossible for one person to withstand if continually exposed to it. It is a steady, incessant pressure, all in one direction. It works night and day. It works all the more efficaciously, because the parent so exposed to it is utterly ignorant of such a force and its operation upon him. He finds himself growing weak. He becomes inert. He lacks his old vigour, and thinks it is through the approach of old age.

I knew a man over seventy years of age and as sound, active and vigorous in mind and body as one of forty. He had organized and built up a large business. His several children at last took it into their heads that it was time " father retired from business." Henceforth, the thought spoken and unspoken, bearing month in and month out on father from the children, was this desire and demand that he should retire from business. Confiding his situation to a friend, he said, "Why should I retire from business? I live in it, I like it, and so far as I can see, am able to conduct it properly." But the persistent demand and force brought to bear on him from these foes of his own blood and household were too great to withstand. He did retire. The sons and daughters were satisfied. The father soon commenced to decline in health. He lived about two years afterwards, and one of his last remarks was, "My children have killed me."

"Ought I not to love my children above all others" asks one. The term " ought " has no application to the nature of love. Love goes where it will, and to whom it will, and where it is attracted. You cannot force yourself to love anything or anybody. There have been parents who had no real love for their children, and children who had no real love for their parents. Neither party can be blamed for this. They were lacking in the capacity for loving. They were born so lacking. They are no more to be censured for such deficiency than you would censure a person for being born blind or cripple.

Some parents fancy they love their children, yet do not. A father who loses his temper and beats his son does not really love that son. It would be better to say that he loved to beat him, or tyrannize over him. Government in the family is necessary; bur no sound, loving government is administered on a basis of anger and irascibility. Parents sometimes interfere and seriously affect the future of a child by opposing its desires in the choice of a profession. The parent may be prejudiced against certain walks in life. The child may wish to follow one of these walks. It meets a bitter, uncompromising opposition on the parent's part. There is no reasoning, discussion, or counselling in the matter--nothing but a stern, positive "No." Such sentiment and act are not impelled by love for the child on the parent's part. They are impelled by the parent's love for his or her own opinion and a love of tyranny.

Parents sometimes forget that after the child emerges from the utter physical and mental helplessness of infancy, it is becoming more and more an individual. As an individual it may show decided tastes, preferences and inclinations in some direction. No parent and no person can break or alter these tastes and preferences. No one can make that child's mind over into something else. For the child's mind as we call it, is really a mind or spirit, which has lived other physical lives from infancy to maturity, if not to old age, and as it comes into possession of its new body, and acquires a relative control over that body, it will begin to act out the man or woman as it was in its former life, and that may be a man or woman very closely related to the parent or hardly related at all. But in any event, the parent is dealing with an individual, who is growing more and more into tastes, preferences, and traits of character which belong to and are a part of it These must have expression. They will have expression in mind or spirit, whether allowed to physically or not. If the boy is ever longing to go to sea, and the parent forbids, the boy is on the sea in mind; and if so in mind, it is far better that his body should follow, for there is only damage when mind and body are not working in correspondence together. If the mother refuse to allow the boy to go to sea because she fears its dangers for him, still she is loving her own fears and her own way, too, more than she does her son.

The parent sometimes usurps a complete tyranny, not only over the child's body, but over its mind. The child's tastes, inclination, tendencies and preferences are held as of no importance whatever. If the boy wants to be a sailor, and the parent wants him something else--that something else the parent may insist that he shall be, but does he succeed? Let the host of mediocrity in all callings in the land answer. And mediocrity means the mechanical following of any pursuit in which there it no live interest.

More than this; where a body is compelled to do one thing, or live in a certain way, and the mind longs to live in another, there is a force set in motion which in many cases tears mind and body apart; and parents sometimes grieve over the loss of a child, when they are responsible for the death of its body from this cause.

How long, then, should parental control continue over the child--or, rather, over a spirit for which you have been an agency for furnishing with a new body? Is it unreasonable to say that such control should not continue after such body, emerging from the helplessness of infancy, shall have acquired such control of its organization as shall enable it to meet all physical demands and necessities? To go beyond this, and give food, clothes, shelter, maintenance, to a person, is doing him or her a great injustice, and even cruelty. In so doing you do not grant exercise to those faculties which must be used in coping successfully with the world. You make the children the less fitted to be self-sustaining, and earn their own living. You teach them to lie in a soft, luxurious bed, when they should be out in the world exercising and making more strong and dexterous their powers, both of mind and body.

Parents sometimes make themselves unjustly responsible, and inflict needless mental suffering on themselves, for the errors and tendencies of their children. A son or daughter takes a wrong course--or, rather, let us put it, a course where the evil is more prominent or more opposed to conventional ideas of propriety than other habits more tolerated and deemed reputable, but which may be the subtle, and for the most part unknown, sources of as great ills as those condemned by society. A son takes to drink or reckless associates and commits some crime. The parent condemns herself for not having looked more carefully after her boy. She may accuse herself as having been, through her neglect, the prime agency for her son's misdeeds.

Madame, you blame yourself far too much. You did not make that son or daughter's character. It was made long before that spirit had the use of its last new body. What traits, what imperfections were very prominent in its last existence, will appear in its next. If that was a thieving spirit before, it will probably show thieving tendencies now. If it was gross, animal and gluttonous, then similar tendencies will show themselves now. You, if grown to a more refined plane of thought, may do much to modify and lessen these tendencies.

But all that you will do in this respect will be done through the silent force and action of your superior thought on your child's mind. It will not be done through a great deal of verbal counsel or physical punishment or discipline.

Whatever a mind is on entering on a new physical experience, whatever imperfection belongs to it, must appear and be acted out and beget pain and punishment of some kind, until that spirit sees clearly for itself, how, through its errors, it brings these punishments on itself. These lessons can only be learned when that person has full freedom, so far as parental control goes, to live as it pleases. You may for a time control such a life, and make it externally live as you please. But such external life is only a veneer, if the mind be full of lower tastes and inclinations. The sooner these are lived out, the sooner will that person learn the real law, which inflicts pains and penalties for breaking its unchangeable rules, and the sooner will it know the happiness which comes of living in accordance with Its rules. That every spirit must do for him or herself.

A parent may mould a false character for a child. It may teach indirectly, through the effect of its own mental condition operating on the child, how to feign what the world calls goodness, how it may seem, as regards outward conduct, to be what it is not at all in secret tendency and inclination,--how, in brief, to be a hypocrite.

No person is really reformed by another, in the sense such a term is sometimes used. Reform must come from within. It must be self-sustaining. It must not depend wholly on another's presence or influence. If it does, it is only a temporary reform. It will fail when the influence of the person on whom it depends is removed. We hear sometimes the assertion, "such or such a person's wife has been the making of him" (meaning the husband). By the way, why do we never hear of the man's being the making of his wife?

A man may be prevented from intemperance, or he may continually be braced up to meet the world through his wife's influence and mental power. But if in such reform he relies entirely upon her; if he cannot sustain himself without her continual presence and prompting, his is no lasting reformation, and he is also a very heavy and damaging load for her to carry. It is a one-sided piece of business when one person must supply all the sustaining force for two, and if this is persisted in, the wife, or whoever so supplies it, will at last sink under such burden, and there will be two wrecked lives instead of one. No person can "make another," in the highest sense. But one person having the superior mind, can, if in a very close and long-continued association with one weaker, give temporarily to the weaker their very life and force, if their desire it very strong to help the weaker. If it be the husband who so receives of the wife, and is so dependent on the wife then he does not represent any character of his own. He represents and is clothed temporarily with his wife's character, or as much of it as he can appropriate. If she dies, or is removed from him, then he relapses and sinks into his real self, unless he is resolved to be self-sustaining, and evolve force out of himself instead of using another's. If she continues to supply him, she is only sustaining his temporary character, which cannot last when its source of supply is removed, and in such continuance she will certainly in time exhaust herself.

Parents often unconsciously teach their children to lie down upon them, to depend upon them too long for moral support. The result of this error is that then the parent's life is dragged out, through carrying so heavy a load, the child ceases to have any genuine love for its parent. You may pity what is decrepit, weak, and shattered. Love it you cannot. Love is based on admiration, and admiration is not compelled by decay.

The tendency called instinct, which impels the mother bird to turn its young out of the nest, so soon as they have sufficient strength to fly, and the animal in weaning its young to turn them adrift and leave them to shift for themselves, is founded on the natural and divine laws. We may say it is the custom of the brutes and is therefore "brutal." But would it be a kindness for the bird to encourage the young to stay in the nest where it could not gain strength, and when a few weeks will bring the storms and severity of winter, which the parent bird itself cannot withstand? Again, the parent, be it bird, animal, or human mother, needs after these periods of bringing their young into the world and rearing them, a season of entire rest and recuperation, and the duration of such resting season should be proportionate to the complexity of the organization and the force expended by such organization. During such periods, the parent should be freed from any and all demands from the child. Birds and animals in their natural or wild life take such periods of rest. But thousands of human mothers are never free from the demands of their children, until worn out they drop into their graves. They should be as free, so far as their children a concerned, as they were in girlhood, and before they became mothers. Motherhood is a most necessary and an indispensable phase of existence for ripening and developing qualities.

But no one experience should be followed and dwelt in forever. Life in its more perfected state will be full of alterations--not a rut, into which if you are once set you must continually travel.

If human children remain with the mother years after attaining what may be termed a responsible age; if they always look to her for aid, advice, sympathy, and assistance; if the mother allows herself to become the family leaning-post, she may also be repeating the one-sided business of supplying too much force to others and getting none back. She may be practising a false and injurious species of motherhood because it is exacted, begged, or dragged from her. She may be robbing herself of the new life which awaits her, when the brood is reared and their wings are self-sustaining. She is helping the children to make her a feeble, witless "old woman."

Perhaps one remarks: " If your suggestion was literally followed, the streets would be full of children turned by parents out of their homes and unable to provide for themselves." So they would. I argue here no literal following of the example set by bird and beast. It would be a great injustice. No custom, when followed for ages, even if based in error, can be suddenly changed without disturbance, injustice, and wrong. Yet it is worth our while to study this principle that we find in nature, from the tree that casts adrift the ripe acorn, to the bird or animal that casts adrift the relatively ripened young. Neither acorn, bird nor animal, when cast off or weaned, ever returns to the parent for self-sustaining power. Such power, in these cases, is only given by the parent until the new organization is strong enough to absorb and appropriate of the elements about it, absorb of earth and sunshine, or flesh or grain, the nourishment necessary to its support.

Are not our streets today full of grown-up children quite unable to provide for themselves? Do not thousands leave parental homes with no self-sustaining power, who are all through life unable to feed, clothe, and shelter themselves, save by long hours of drudging labour at the lowest wages? Does not this life of drudgery exhaust and cut them off prematurely? Are there not thousands of daughters all over the land who will become "old maids," and whose parents will not permit them, were they so disposed, to go out in the world and take their chances? These are the birds cuddled in the nest, until their wings, denied exercise, lose at last all power or prompting for flight, and whose mouths, though they become grown-up birds, are trained only to open and receive the morsels dropped in them.

Chapter 3: Thought Currents

We need to be careful of what we think and talk. Because thought runs in currents as real as those of air and water. Of what we think and talk we attract to us a like current of thought. This acts on mind or body for good or ill.

If thought was visible to the physical eye we should see its currents flowing to and from people. We should see that persons similar in temperament, character and motive are in the same literal current of thought. We should see that the person in a despondent and angry mood was in the same current with others despondent or angry, and that each one in such moods serves as an additional battery or generator of such thought and is strengthening that particular current. We should see these forces working in similar manner and connecting the hopeful, courageous and cheerful, with all others hopeful, courageous and cheerful.

When you are in low spirits or "blue" you have acting on you the thought current coming from all others in low spirits. You are in oneness with the despondent order of thought. The mind is then sick. It can be cured, but a permanent cure cannot always come immediately when one has long been in the habit of opening the mind to this current of thought.

In attracting to us the current of any kind of evil, we become for a time one with evil. In the thought current of the Supreme Power for good we may become more and more as one with that power, or in Biblical phrase "One with God." That is the desirable thought current for us to attract.

If a group of people talk of any form of disease or suffering, of death-bed scenes and dying agonies, if they cultivate this morbid taste for the unhealthy and ghastly, and it forms their staple topics of conversation, they bring in themselves a like current of thought full of images of sickness, suffering and things revolting to a healthy mind. This current will act on them, and eventually bring them disease and suffering in some form.

If we are talking much of sick people or are much among them and thinking of them, be our motive what it may, we shall draw on ourselves a current of sickly thought, and its ill results will in time materialize itself in out bodies. We have far more to do to save ourselves than is now realized.

When men talk business together they attract a business current of idea and suggestion. The better they agree the more of this thought current do they attract and the more do they receive of idea and suggestion for improving and extending their business. In this way does the conference or discussion among the leading members of the company or corporation create the force that carries their business ahead.

Travel in first-class style, put up at first-class hotels and dress in apparel "as costly as your purse can buy," without running into the extreme of foppishness. In these things you find aids to place you in a current of relative power and success. If your purse does not now warrant such expenditure, or you think it does not, you can commence so living in mind. This will make you take the first steps in this direction. Successful people in the domain of finance unconsciously live up to this law. Desire for show influences some to this course. But there is another force and factor which so impels them. That is a wisdom of which their material minds are scarcely conscious. It is the wisdom of the spirit telling them to get in the thought current of the successful, and by such current be borne to success. It is not a rounded-out success, but good is far as it goes.

If our minds are, from what is falsely called economy, ever set on the cheap--cheap lodgings, cheap food and cheap fares, we get in the thought current of the cheap, the slavish and the fearful. Our views of life and our plans will be influenced and warped by it. It paralyzes that courage and enterprise implied in the old adage "Nothing ventured nothing gained." Absorbed in this current and having it ever acting on you, it is felt immediately when you come into the presence of the successful and causes them to avoid you. They feel in you the absence of that element which brings them their relative success. It acts as a barrier, preventing the flow to you of their sympathy. Sympathy is a most important factor in business. Despite opposition and competition, a certain thought current of sympathy binds the most successful together. The mania for cheapness lies in the thought current of fear and failure. The thought current of fear and failure, and the thought current of dash, courage and success will not mingle nor bring together the individuals who are in these respective streams of thought. They antagonize, and between the two classes of mind is built a barrier more impenetrable than walls of stone.

Live altogether in any one idea, any one "reform" and you get into the thought current of all other minds who are carrying that idea to extremes. There is no "reform" but what can be pushed too far. The harm of such extreme falls on the person who so pushes it. It warps mind, judgment and reason all on one side. It makes fanatics, bigots, cranks and lunatics, whether the idea involves an art or study, a science, a "reform" or a "movement." It connects the extremists of all people in such order and current of mind, no matter what their specialties may be. Such people often end in becoming furious haters of all who differ with them and in so hating expend their force in tearing themselves to pieces. The safe side lies in calling daily for the thought current of wisdom from the Infinite Mind.

When that wisdom is more invoked our "reforms" and organizations "for the good of the whole" will not run into internal wrangles almost as soon as they organize. As now conducted the thought current of hatred of and antagonism to the "oppressor" and monopolist is admitted at their birth. This very force breeds quarrels and dissensions among the members. It is force used to tear down instead of build up. It is like taking the fire used to generate steam in the boilers and scattering it throughout the building.

When people come together and in any way talk out their ill-will towards others they are drawing to themselves with ten-fold power an injurious thought current. Because the more minds united on any purpose the more power do they attract to effect that purpose. The thought current so attracted by those chronic complainers, grumblers and scandal mongers, will injure their bodies. Because whatever thought is most held in mind is most materialized in the body. If we are always thinking and talking of people's imperfections we are drawing to us ever of that thought current, and thereby incorporating into ourselves those very imperfections.

We have said in previous books that "Talk Creates Force," and that the more who talk in sympathy the greater is the volume and power of the thought current generated and attracted for good or ill. A group of gossips who can never put their heads together without raking over the faults of the absent are unconsciously working a law with terrible results to themselves.

Gossip is fascinating. There is an exhilaration in scandal and the raking over of our friend's or neighbour's or enemy's faults is almost equal to that produced by champagne. But in the end we pay dearly for these pleasures.

If but two people were to meet at regular intervals and talk of health, strength and vigour of body and mind, at the same time opening their minds to receive of the Supreme the best idea as to the ways and means for securing these blessings, they would attract to them a thought current of such idea. If these two people or more kept up these conversations on these subjects at a regular time and place, and found pleasure in such communings, and they were not forced or stilted; if they could carry them on without controversy, and enter into them without preconceived idea, and not allow any shade of tattle or tale-bearing, or censure of others to drift into their talk, they would be astonished at the year's end at the beneficial results to mind and body. Because in so doing and coming together with a silent demand of the Supreme to get the best idea, they would attract to them a current of Life-giving force.

Let two so commence rather than more. For even two persons in the proper agreement and accord to bring the desired results are not easy to find. The desire for such meetings must be spontaneous, and any other motive will bar out the highest thought current for good.

The old-fashioned revival meeting, or camp meeting, through the combined action and desire of a number of minds brought a thought current, causing for the time the ecstasy, fervour and enthusiasm which characterized those gatherings The North American Indian worked himself into the frenzy of his war dance by a similar law. He brought to him by force of united desire a thought element and current which stimulated and even intoxicated him. His sole desire was to bring on him this mental intoxication. The more minds so working in the same vein, the quicker came the desired result.

The real orator in his effort draws to him a current of thought, which as sent again from him to his audience, thrills them. So does the inspired actor or actress. They bring a higher and more powerful element of thought to themselves first, and this flowing through them acts on the audience afterwards.

If you dwell a great deal on your own faults you will by the same laws attract more and more of their thought current, and so increase those faults. It is enough that you recognize in yourself those faults. Don't be always saying of yourself, "I am weak or cowardly or ill-tempered or imprudent," Draw to yourself rather the thought current of strength, courage, even temper, prudence and all other good qualities. Keep the image of these qualities in mind and you make them a part of yourself.

You have sometimes been beset, absorbed, and even annoyed for days in the thought of the suit of clothes you wanted to buy, the cut, colour and fashion of a dress, the selection of a bonnet, or cravat, until you were nothing in thought but clothes, hat, bonnet, dress, cravat or some other detail of life. You may not have been able to make up your mind what you should buy, and have then possibly been tossed about mentally on the billows of indecision for days. You have then got into the thought current of thousands of other minds continually in this mood of thought.

The surest way for a young woman to become ugly is to be discontented, peevish, cross, complaining and envious of others. Because in these states of mind she is drawing to her the invisible substance of thought, which acts on and injures her body. It ruins the complexion, makes lines and creases in the face, sharpens the nose and transforms the face of youth into that of the shrew in very quick time.

I am not moralizing here or saying: "You ought not to do thus and so." It is simply cause and result. Put your face in the fire, and it is scarred and disfigured, because of an element acting on it. Put your mind in the fire of ill-will, envy or jealousy, and it is also scarred, seamed and disfigured, because of an element as real as fire, though invisible, acting on it.

All things that are evil and imperfect, such as disagreeable traits of character in others--things unpleasant to hear or look upon should be gotten out of our minds as quickly as possible. Otherwise if dwelt upon, they attract of their thought current. They will then become permanent spiritual fixtures, and these will in time materialize themselves into corresponding physical fixtures. If we are always keeping in mind the person doing some wrong thing, we are the more apt to do that very thing ourselves.

Let us endeavour, then, with the help of the Supreme Power, to get into the thought current of things that are healthy, natural, strong and beautiful. Let us try to avoid thoughts of disease, of suffering, of deformity, of faultiness. A field of waving grain or the rolling surf is better to contemplate than to pore over the horrors of a railway accident. We do not realize how much we are depressed physically and mentally by the incessant feast of horrors prepared for us by the daily press. We invoke in their perusal a thought current, filled with things and images of horror and suffering. We bring ourselves in this way in connection and one-ness with all other morbid and diseased mind, which lives and revels in this current. it leads not to life, but to disease and death. Neither others nor yourself are one particle aided by your knowing of every fire, explosion, murder, theft or crime which the newspapers chronicle every twenty-fours hours.

If we read boots written by cynical, sarcastic minds, who are so warped as to be able to see only the faults of others, and at last unable to see good anywhere, we bring on ourselves their unhealthy thought current, and are one with it. The arrow always tipped with ill-nature and sarcasm is deadliest to him who sends it. In other words, the man who is ever inviting and cultivating this thought current, is inviting the unrest, disease and misfortune it will assuredly bring to him, and when we get too much into his mind we invite similar results.

You may be neat, careful and methodical in your habits, exact and elaborate in your work, yet if you associate closely with those who are careless and slovenly you may find in yourself a tendency to be also careless and slovenly, and a difficulty in resuming and carrying out your former neat, methodical and orderly methods. Because you have not only absorbed of the careless mind, or the mind lacking patience to do anything reposefully, but the fragment of such mind so absorbed is acting as a magnet in attracting to you its like thought current.

When an evil is known it is half cured. Bear in mind when you are in any unpleasant frame of mind that a thought current of such disagreeable mood is acting on you. Bear in mind that you are then one in a sort of electrical connection with many other sickly and morbid minds, all generating and sending unpleasant thought to each other. The next thing to be done is to pray or demand to get out of this current of evil thought. You cannot do this wholly of your own individual effort. You must demand of the Supreme Power to divert it from you.

We can more and more invite the thought current of things that are lively, sprightly and amusing. Life should be full of playfulness. Continued seriousness is but a few degrees removed front gloom and melancholy. Thousands live too much in the thought current of seriousness. Faces which wear a smiling expression are scarce. Some never smile at all. Some have forgotten how to smile, and it actually hurts them to smile, or to see others do so. Sickness and disease are nursed into fresher and fresher activity by the serious mood of mind. Habit continually strengthens the sad capacity of dwelling on the malady, which may be the merest trifle at first. People get so much in this current that woeful diseases are manufactured out of some trifling irritation in some part of the body.

Many material things are helps to divert a thought current acting disagreeably on you. You may have daily a set of disagreeable symptoms. They may seem to come as adjuncts to the daily routine of life. The breakfast table, the furniture, the conversation and even the persons immediately about you seem to recall them. Travel sometimes banishes them entirely. The sight of different surroundings diverts that particular thought current. Material remedies may temporarily effect the same result. So may any sudden change of life or occupation. But all these are secondary aids to the Supreme Power.

The thought current of fear is everywhere. All humanity fears something--disease, death, loss of fortune, loss of friends, loss of something. Everyone has his or her pet fear. It extends to the most trivial details of life. The streets are full of people who, if fearing nothing else, fear they won't catch a train or the next street car. The more sensitive you are to the impress of thought, the more liable are you to be affected by this thought current of fear until your spirit, by constant demand of the Supreme Power, builds up for itself an armour of thought positive to this current, and one which will deny it access. You can commence this building in saying, whenever you are affected in the way above mentioned, or in any disagreeable fashion, "I refuse to accept this thought and the mental condition it has brought on me which affects my body." You commence then to turn aside the thought current of evil.

Everyone has some pet fear--some disease they may never have had, but always dreaded-- something they are in special fear of losing. Some trifle, even but a word or sentence uttered by another, brings this pet fear to the mind. Instantly through long habit the minds reverts to this fear. Instantly it opens to it, and the whole thought, volume and current rushes to and acts on them. It acts and vibrates on that particular chord of your nature, which for years has sounded your pet weakness.

Then in some way the body is affected disagreeably. There are myriads of different symptoms. The body may become weak and tremulous. There may be loss of appetite, tremulousness, a dry tongue, a bad taste in the mouth, weakness in the joints, drowsiness, difficulty of concentrating the mind on your business and many other disagreeable sensations.

Such symptoms are often classed as " malaria." In a sense the name is a correct one. Only in very many of these cases it is a bad atmosphere or current of thought which is acting on our minds instead of the fancied bad material atmosphere. Unquestionably an atmosphere full of vegetable or animal decomposition will affect many people. But some live for years in the midst of stagnant pools and swamps who never have malaria. Others far removed from such locations on high and dry ground do have it. They hare taken on a thought current of fear.

Place yourself in a house where there has recently been a panic or scare, though you may know nothing of it. You were well and strong the day before. You arise in the morning, and soon this whole train of disagreeable sensations affects you, because the house or place is saturated with a thought current of fear. Put a fear on city, town or country of some deadly epidemic or some great calamity, and hundreds of the more sensitive who may have no fear of that epidemic or calamity are still affected by it disagreeably. That thought current affects them in their particular a weak spot. A fanatic predicts some great catastrophe. The sensational newspapers take up the topic, ventilate it, affect to ridicule, but still write about it. This sets more minds to thinking and more people to talking. The more talk the more of this injurious force is generated. As a result thousands of people are affected by it unpleasantly, some in one way, some in another, because the whole force of that volume of fear is let loose upon them. Some are killed outright. Entirely unaware of the cause, they open their minds more and more to it, dwell on it in secret, put out no resisting thought until at last the spirit, unable longer to carry such a load, snaps the link which connects it with the body.

The more impressionable you are to the thought about you the more are you liable to be thus affected. But you can train your mind to shut out this thought. You can gradually train it to bar tightly this door to weakness, and keep open only the one to strength. You can do this by cultivating the mood of drawing to yourself and keeping in the mood and current of thought coming of God or the Supreme Power for good.

Impressionability or capacity to receive thought is source either of strength or weakness. Fine-grained, sensitive, highly developed minds today often carry the weakest bodies, because through ignorance they are always inviting some of these currents of evil without any knowledge of their existence or the means of throwing them off. They are ignorantly either courting or exposing themselves to such current. Improper individual association is one chief source of such exposure.

The finer feminine organization is more sensitive to every shade and ray of thought about it, good or bad. Men absorbed in their business generate for a time a certain positiveness which throws off the fear current. But this positiveness cannot always last.

Women from this cause often suffer a thousandfold more in the privacy of their homes than men are aware of. The average man defines it as " woman's way," and wonders why she is so full of " nervousness," " vapours," "notions," and ill-health.

As you place your reliance on the Infinite Mind to bring you out of all these agencies for ill, that mind in some way will bring many material aids to help you out. That mind will suggest medicines and foods and surroundings and changes, not only to help you temporarily, but permanently, so that when you are cured you are cured for all time. A cheerful, buoyant, hopeful mind (and no mind is cheerful, hopeful and buoyant without being nearer the Infinite than one that is depressed, sour and gloomy), be that the mind of your doctor, or your friend, will help you to get out of the injurious thought current. Regard such mind as a help from the Infinite. But don't put your whole trust in that individual. Put the great trust in the Supreme Power which has sent to you the individual as a temporary aid or crutch until your spiritual limbs are strong enough to bear you.

The more you get into the thought current coming from the Infinite Mind, making yourself more and more a part of that mind (exactly as you may become a part of any vein of low, morbid, unhealthy mind in opening yourself to that current), the quicker are you freshened, and renewed physically and mentally. You become continually a newer being. Changes for the better come quicker and quicker. Your power increases to bring results. You lose gradually all fear as it is proven more and more to you that when you are in the thought current of Infinite good there is nothing to fear. You realize more and more clearly that there is a great power and force which cares for you. You are wonderstruck at the fact that when your mind is set in the right direction all material things come to you with very little physical or external effort. You wonder then at man's toiling and striving, fagging himself literally to death, when through such excess of effort he actually drives from him the rounded-out good of health, happiness and material prosperity all combined.

You will see in this demand for the highest good that you are growing to power greater than you ever dreamed of. It will dawn on you that the real life destined for the awakened few now, and the many in the future is a dazzling dream--a permanent realization that it is a happiness to exist--a serenity and contentment without abatement--a transition from pleasure to pleasure, and from the great to the greater pleasure. You find as you get more and more into the current of the Infinite Mind that exhausting toil is not required of you, but that when you commit yourself in trust to this current and let it bear you where it will, all things needful will come to you.

When you are getting into the right thought current, you may for a time experience more of uneasiness, physical and mental than ever. This is because the new element acting on you makes you more sensitive to the presence of evil. The new is driving the old out. The new thought current searches and detects every little error in your mind before unnoticed, and repels it. This causes a struggle, and mind and body are for a time unpleasantly affected by it. It is like house-cleaning, a process usually involving a good deal of dust and disturbance. The new spirit you call to you is cleaning your spiritual house.

There is no limit to the power of the thought current you can attract to you nor limit to the things that can he done through the individual by it. In the future some people will draw so much of the higher quality of thought to them, that by it they will accomplish what some would call miracles. In this capacity of the human mind for drawing a thought current ever increasing in fineness of quality and power lies the secret of what has been called "magic."

Chapter 4: One Way to Cultivate Courage

Courage and presence of mind mean the same thing. Presence of mind implies command of mind. Cowardice and lack of mental control mean about the same thing. Cowardice is rooted in hurry, the habit of hurry or lack of repose. All degrees of success are based on courage--mental or physical. All degrees of failure are based on timidity.

You can cultivate courage and increase it at every minute and hour of the day. You can have the satisfaction of knowing that in everything you do you have accomplished two things--namely, the doing of the thing itself and by the manner of its doing, adding eternally to yourself another atom of the quality of courage. You can do this by the cultivation of deliberation--deliberation of speech, of walk, of writing, of eatlng--deliberation in everything.

There is always a bit of fear where there is a bit of hurry. When you hurry to the train you are in fear that you may be left, and with that comes fear of other possibilities consequent on your being left. When you hurry to the party, to the meeting of a person by appointment, you are in fear of some ill or damage resulting from not being in time.

This habit of thought can, through an unconscious training, grow to such an extent as to pervade a person's mind, at all times and places, and bring on a fear of loss of some kind, when there is absolutely no loss to be sustained. For instance a person may hurry to catch a street car and act and feel as if a great loss would occur did he not get on that particular car, when there may be another close behind, or at most two or three minutes' waiting will bring it. Yet the fear of waiting those three minutes grows to a mountain in size, and is in that person's mind a most disagreeable possibility. Through mere habit a similar condition of hurry may characterize that person's walking, eating, writing--in short, everything he does, and will render it more and more difficult for such person to act with coolness and deliberation.

The quality of mind or emotion underlying all this hurried mental condition and consequent hurried act, is fear. Fear is but another name for lack of power to control our minds, or, in other words, to control the kind of thought we think or put out.

It is this kind of unconscious mental training (which is very common), that begets a permanent condition of mind more and more liable to large and small panics at the least interruption or trivial disappointment. It makes disappointments when none are necessary. It is the ever- opening wedge letting in more and more the thought current of fear. For if you so cultivate fear of one thing you are cultivating and increasing liability to fear in all things. If you allow yourself to sit in fear for half an hour that the carriage may not call for you in time to get to the boat or train, you are much more liable to be seized with a series of little panics at every trivial occurrence or obstacle occurring on that particular journey.

In this way does this habit of mind enter into and is cultivated in the doing of so-called little things. You are writing or sewing, or engaged in the performance of some work which is intensely interesting to you, and in which you do not like to be interrupted. If sewing, you reach for your scissors which have dropped on the floor. You do this in a momentarily impatient mood and with a spasmodic jerky action. Your mind, as the phrase runs, is "on your work." You will not take it off your work while reaching for the scissors. You are trying in mind to go on with your work and reach for the scissors at the same moment. You make the movement of muscles and the action of the body momentarily disagreeable and irksome, because you refuse for the second to put into that act the force which it demands. When unconsciously you refuse to do this, any acts will become irksome and disagreeable, because there is not force enough let on to do the act with ease. It is the endeavour to do it with a weak body. You have the power of throwing your force instantly into any muscle, so making the act easy and pleasant. This capacity for turning on force on any part you will increases through cultivating it. And you can do a great deal more and do it better through this cultivation of deliberation, for deliberation can be as quick as thought, the more the mind is trained in that direction.

If you pick up a pin or tie a shoe-string in a hurry, you do so not only because such act is irksome to you, but because you fear it may deprive you momentarily of some bit of pleasure. There you have again opened your mind to the thought current of fear--fear of losing something.

The cultivation of courage commences in the cultivation of deliberation in so-called little acts like these. Deliberation and courage are as closely allied as fear and hurry. If we do not learn to govern our force properly in the doing of the smallest act we shall find such government far less easy in the doing of all acts.

If we analyze what we fear, we shall find we are in mind trying to deal with too much at once of the thing feared. There is only a relatively small amount to be dealt with now. In any transaction --in the doing of anything there is but one step to be taken at a time. We need to place what force is necessary, and no more on that one step. When that is taken we can take the next.

The more we train our minds so to concentrate on the one step, the more do we increase capacity for sending our force all in one given direction at once. Such force extends, and should be so used in the so-called minutest details of everyday life. In this way deliberation and deliberate action become habitual, and we are in a sense unconscious of making ourselves deliberate, even as after long training in the opposite and wrong direction we are unconscious of putting on the hurried frame of mind.

Timidity is often the result of looking at too many difficulties or terrors at once. In material reality we have to deal with but one at a time. If we are going to what we fear will be a disagreeable interview with a harsh, irascible, over-bearing person, we are apt to go, occupying our minds with the whole interview, setting ourselves down in the very middle of it, and seeing it in mind as necessarily trying or disagreeable. Perhaps we were thinking of it this morning while we were dressing. But it was then our proper business to dress. To dress was a necessary step for the interview and to dress well also. Possibly it occupied our thoughts while eating. But it was then our proper business to eat and get all the pleasure possible from our food. That was another step. The more reposeful our eating, the more vigorous will become our taste, and the more strength will our food give our bodies. Possibly the fear of this interview was on us as we walked to the place appointed for it. But it was then our proper business to walk and get from our walking all the pleasure he could. That was another step. Pleasure is the sure result of placing thought or force on the thing we are doing now, and pain of some sort in both present and future is the certain result of sending thought or force away from the act which needs to be done at this moment.

When we dress, eat, walk or do anything with mind placed on something else, we are making the present act irksome; we are training to make every act irksome and disagreeable; we are making the thing feared a certainty, for what we put out in thought as unpleasant is an actual thing, a reality. And the longer we continue to put it out the more force we add to it, and the more likely is it then to be realized in the physical world.

To bring us what all want and are seeking for, namely-happiness, we need to have perfect control of our mind and thought at all times and places. One most important and necessary means for gaining this, lies in this discipline regarding so-called little or trivial things, just as the discipline and movement of an army commences with the training of the private soldiers' legs and arms. If you hurry and slur over these so-called petty details, you are the easier thrown off your guard or confused at unexpected occurrences, and in life it is the unexpected that is always happening.

We need to keep always our mind present with us. We want it always on the spot ready to use in any direction. Our thought is not on the spot when we tie a shoe-string and think a mile from that shoe-string--when we mend a pencil and dwell in one of tomorrow's cares. It is then away, and if it has for a lifetime been in the habit of so straying from the act in hand to the act afar, it becomes more and more difficult to bring it back to use, and more difficult to use it promptly when it is brought back. Our thought moves from one thing to another with more than electric speed, and we can unconsciously train this quickness to be ever darting from one thing to another until it becomes almost impossible to keep it on one thing for ten consecutive seconds. On the contrary, through cultivation of repose and deliberation in all things we can train ourselves to mass and fasten our thought on anything as long as we please, to throw ourselves into any mood of mind we please, and to throw ourselves at will into sleep or a semi-conscious, dreamy state as restful as sleep. These are very small parts of the possibilities for the human mind. There is no limit to its growth or the increase of its power, and no thing coming within the limits of our imagination but can be accomplished by it. The steps to these attainments are very small, very simple and relatively easy--so simple and easy that some reject them for that reason.

Unquestionably, these powers and many results coming of their exercise were known ages ago to a relative few. But any power or any condition of mind consequent upon it can be made more clear to an English-speaking people, through the use of an English word or form of expression than by terms taken from other languages.

The North American Indian and the Oriental had in cases the power of so dismissing all thought and making their minds in a sense a blank as to become not only insensible to fear, but this mental condition rendered their bodies almost insensible to physical suffering. It was the power of inducing this mental condition which enabled the Indian when taken captive to withstand every device of torture inflicted by his captors, and to sing his death song under the infliction of fire and a slow process of bodily mutilation too horrible for description, and which very few of our race could endure without passing into the frenzy of agony.

The Indian is far more reposeful and deliberate than the majority of our race, in both mental and physical movement. Unconsciously cultivating this repose. and living a life less artificial than ours, he increased his spiritual power, one sure result of which is that command of mind over body which can lessee physical pain, and as an ultimate possibility banish it altogether.

Deliberation of movement, or in plainer English movement of muscle so slow that our mind has time to follow it, gives one time to think in great and small emergencies. But the lack of such training causes unconscious physical action. So confirmed becomes this habit, that the body moves without us aware of it. Awkwardness, lack of address, lack of tact are all due to this lack of command of mind caused by lack of deliberation, or in other words, a trained incapacity for taking time to think or plan the proper thing to do.

The terror-stricken person if the ship seems in sudden danger runs up and down the deck to no purpose, and this physical action is an exact correspondence of the life-long condition of his mind whose thought has been ever so darting from one thing to another, just as the whim seized him.

The more deliberate person whose mind is trained to take time to think and hold or concentrate its thought, holds himself steady, and so gives himself time to see what may be the opportunities for escape. And these two persons would pick up a pin in a very different manner and with very different mental action and method.

To train then for courage is to train for deliberate movement in all things, for that is simply training to mass and hold your force in reserve and let out no more than is needed for the moment.

No quality of mind is more needful to success in all undertakings than courage, and by courage I mean not only courage to act but courage to think. In everyday business, thousands dare not think of taking a step which would involve an outlay of money above the average of their expenditure. They are appalled at mention of so large a sum. They will not, out of pure fright, entertain the idea long enough to familiarize themselves with it. Now if they reversed this mental action, and instead of immediately giving way out of life-long habit to this fright, would take time and allow the thought to rest in their minds instead of driving it out, there would in time come to them ideas concerning ways and means for meeting the additional expense, and thereby making a larger sum of money in the same time it took to make the small sum.

For instance, you say to the women who goes out to wash by the day and has never done anything else. "Mrs. A., why don't you start a laundry? You can make a great deal more money in so doing."

"I start a laundry! Where in the world is the money coming from to start a laundry?" is her reply. Here the woman instead of entertaining your idea gives way immediately to fright concerning what seems to her the immense sum required, and following the same unreasoning, headlong, panicky style of thought, sets up in a moment an opposition to your proposition. She dare think only of working for day's wages as she is called upon by those who hire her. And thousands for this reason dare not think, or find it disagreeable for them to think, of getting into some broader, more responsible and more profitable sphere of business, because they bunch at once all its possible difficulties into a mass, and out of mere habit will look only at that awful and imaginary bunch.

But Mrs. C., the more deliberate washerwoman, hears your proposition and entertains it. In time she says to herself, "Why should I not start a laundry? Other people have and have succeeded." She lives in the idea, talks to one and another about it, and finds out how they started. The longer she keeps in this current of thought the more plainly does she see the ways and means by which other people have "set up for themselves." Finally, the idea so grows upon her, that she takes some step toward that end, and then another and another, and so by degrees drifts into the business.

A person is cool and collected in face of any great danger, because he has the power of holding his mind to the thing to be done on the instant. Cowardice has no such power, and can see in mind not only the source of danger, but a score of possible results which may or may not happen to him. In battle one man may attend to his duty with a vivid and by no means agreeable condition of mind as he sees men struck and mangled all about him. But the force or thought he can bring to bear on the performance of his duty is greater in amount than that coming of the realization of the slaughter around him, and commands and holds his body to his post. The man who runs, or would if he had the chance, cannot fix his mind on anything but the fearful possibilities of the moment.

In the so-called trivial act of picking up a pin, or threading a needle, or opening a door, I do not argue that all one's force or thought should be placed on the act, but only enough to perform the act well while the rest is kept in reserve. It is in substance the same as in picking up a weight, you would not try to expend the force in lifting one pound that you would in lifting fifty pounds. You do expend a great deal more force in the act of picking up a pin when your mind is preoccupied with something else, for you are then trying to do two things or lift two weights at once.

You will remember that anything which is done in mind, expends quite as much force as if done with the body, so that the persons who linger abed in the morning and think with dread of the breakfasts to be cooked, or the rooms to be swept, so far as expenditure of force is concerned, will be doing those acts then and there while lying on their backs.

In expending just force enough to perform any act (a capacity which will gradually grow upon you as you familiarize yourself with this idea and set your desire or demand upon it,) you cultivate and increase continually that desirable state of mind, which in everyday language is known as "having your wits about you." That means, in other words, always having, no matter what you are doing, your mental eyes open in every direction, and while outwardly you seem all intent and occupied in the one act, your mind or spirit like a vigilant sentinel is continually on the look-out, so as to give you notice in the fractional part of an instant of all that is going on about you, and also to direct you how to meet the event whatever it may be. This is not only the characteristic of courage, but of tact and address. It was this electric vigilance and mind watchfulness that gave an American officer during the Revolution, who, in the confusion of battle, suddenly found himself in front of a British regiment, the deliberation to ask, "What troops are these?" "The Royal Scots," was the reply. " Royal Scots remain as you are," was his answer, and he rode off to his own lines. That man had a mind trained to give him time to think.

On one occasion, Mrs. Farren, the celebrated English actress, discovered where her part required her to hem a handkerchief that the property man had forgotten to lay out the handkerchief needle, thread, etc. Without a moment's hesitation she sat down and imitated so naturally the motion and manner of a lady in sewing that most of her audience never suspected the omission. That act involved self possession, coolness, deliberation, presence of mind, courage. Do not all these terms imply a similar state of mind? A woman habitually hurried and flurried could not have done this, and I believe that when Mrs. Farren saw proper to pick up a pin, she did so in a much more deliberate manner than would the habitually hurried, flurried man or woman.

Cultivate deliberate act and movement in all things, and you lay more and more the solid foundation for courage, either moral or physical. But deliberate act does not always imply slowness. Just as thought moves with electric rapidity, so may it move the body when occasion requires, but the thought must be clearly planned, seen and outlined in mind before it is allowed to act on the body. It is so seen or planned, and so acts to use the muscles in the rapid thrust and parry of the skilled fencer, and similarly with the professional danseuse, in fact in all superior accomplishments, be they of painter, musician or other artist. These, however, in many cases, are but partial controls of mind. Outside of his art, the artist may have little mental control or deliberation, and as a result be "nervous" vacillating, easily disturbed, whimsical and timid. The mind is our garrison to be armed at all points and disciplined to meet any emergency.

We deal with the making (or self-making) of whole men and women, whose minds are not cultivated all in one direction and neglected everywhere else. It is far better in the end to be growing symmetrically and to be finished so far as we have grown "all around," than to have our power all concentrated on one talent or capacity, and becoming what the world calls a "Genius." The inside history of Genius is often a sad one, and shows that it brought little happiness to its possessor.

Scores and hundreds of the little acts of everyday life, such as picking dropped articles from the floor, opening and shutting drawers, laying or reaching for articles on the toilet table, and attending to minor details of dress, are done unconsciously in this hurried condition of mind, especially when some more important object engages our attention. We snatch, we clutch, we drive recklessly about in the doing of these things, and we weaken our bodies and become tired out, and finally "panicky," and easily frightened through this mental habit, for fear and cowardice slip in far more easily when the body is weak.

This habit cannot be changed in a day or a year when it has pervaded a lifetime. Neither can the ills, mental and physical, resulting from such habit, be cured immediately. There can be only gradual growth away from them.

If in reading this you feel convinced that there is "something in it," and feel also a conviction that some portion of it suits your own case, your cure has then commenced. Real conviction, the conviction that comes from within, never leaves one or stops working to get us out of the evil way and put us in the good one. It may seem buried and forgotten for seasons, and our erroneous habits may seem growing stronger than ever. That is not so. But as convictions take root we are seeing our errors more and more clearly. We forget that at one time we were blind and did not see them at all.

If this book brings to you a conviction of a long established error it is not I individually who bring or convince. It is only that I put out more or less of a truth, which takes hold of you and the chord of truth in you senses it. If I apply the torch to the gas-jet and light it, it does not follow that I make either the fire or the gas. I am only a means or agent for lighting that gas. No man makes or invents a truth. Truth is as general and widely spread and belongs to every individual as much as the air we breathe, and there is pleasure enough in being its torch-bearer without presuming to claim the power of its Creator.

Above all demand more and more courage of the Supreme Power.

Chapter 5: Look Forward!

The tendency with many people after they are a little "advanced in years" is to look backward and with regret. The "looking" should be the other way--forward. If you want to go backward in every sense, mental and physical, keep on cultivating the mood of living regretfully in your past life.

It is one chief characteristic of the material mind to hold tenaciously to the past. It likes to recall the past and mourn over it. The material mind has a never-ending series of solemn amusement, in recalling past joys, and feeling sad because they are never to come again.

But the real self, the spirit, cares relatively little for its past. it courts change. II expects to be a different individual in thought a year hence from that it is today. It is willing a thousand years hence to forget who or what it is today, for it knows that this intense desire to remember itself for what it has been retards its advance toward greater power and greater pleasure. What care you for what you were a thousand or five thousand years ago? Yet then you were something, and something far less than what you are today. You are curious you may answer to know what you were. Yes, but is curiosity worth gratifying, if for such gratification you must pay the price of dragging after you a hundred corpses of your dead selves. Those selves, those existences, have done their work for you. In doing that work they brought you possibly more pain than pleasure. Do you want ever to bear with you the memory and burden of that pain? Especially when such burden brings more pain and deprives you of pleasure. It is like the bird that should insist on carrying with it always the shell from which it was hatched. If you have a sad remembrance fling it off. If you can't fling it off, demand of the Supreme Power aid to help you do so, and such aid will come. If you want to grow old, feeble, gray and withered, go at once and live in your past, and regret your youth. Go and to revisit places and houses where you lived twenty, thirty, forty years ago; call back the dead; mourn over them; live in remembrance over the joys you had there, and say they are gone and fled and will never come again.

In so doing you are fastening dead selves all over you. If we came into another physical life with the memory of the last one, we should come into the world physically as miniature, decrepit, grizzled old men and women. Youth physically is fresh and blooming, because it packs no past sad material remembrances with it. A girl is beautiful because her spirit has flung off the past and sad remembrance of its previous life, and has therefore a chance for a period to assert itself. A woman commences to "age" then she commences to load up with regrets over a past but twenty years gone.

Your spirit demands for the body it uses grace, agility of movement and personal beauty, for it is made in the "image of God," and the infinite mind and life, beauty, grace and agility are the characteristics of that mind. In that phase of existence we called childhood and youth, the spirit has the chance to assert its desire for beauty and agility, because it has not as yet loaded up with false beliefs and regrets.

The liveliness, sprightliness and untiring playfulness of the boy or girl of ten or twelve, is due to the gladness of spirit relieved of the burden that is carried in a past existence. That burden was one of thoughts unprofitable to carry. You would physically have the agility you had at fifteen could you fling off the burden of sad remembrance and belief in error that you have been loading up with these twenty or thirty years past.

You can commence the unloading process now, by resolving, with the aid of the Supreme Power, to fling off the remembrance of everything in the past that has annoyed you, everything you regret, everything you have mourned over.

God never mourns or regrets. You as a spirit are made in His image. God it eternal life, joy and serenity. The more of these characteristics you reflect the nearer are you to the Infinite Spirit of Good.

Have you buried your dearest on earth? You do them no good by your sad thoughts concerning them. You place bar twixt their spirit and yours in thinking of them as "lost." You may in so doing not only increase and encourage in them a sad mental condition, but bring their gloomy mental condition on yourself, as many do in grieving. The greatest good we can do them is to think of them as alive like ourselves, and to fling their graves, tombstones, coffins, shrouds and ghastliness out of our minds. If we cannot do so of ourselves let us demand help of the Supreme Power to do it. We often make those who have lost their bodies feel dead when we think of them as such. If we do this they will throw back their thoughts of deadness on us.

Keep out of graveyards. It may seem to some that I am cold and unfeeling to say thus, but the truth, as it presents itself to me, says that the graveyard where your loved ones do not lie, is spiritually a most unhealthy place to visit. They are full of the thought of regret, death and decay. When you visit them you incorporate such thought into yourself. It is hostile and killing to youth, vigour, elasticity, cheerfulness and life.

Our graveyards are full of lies, We place a stone over the cast-off body of a friend. We place on that stone the word "died." That is not true. Your friend is not dead. It is only the body he used that lies there. But that grave is planted in your memory, and your friend in your mind lies in it. Do what we will, try to believe what we may of the eternal prolongation of life and the impossibility of anything like death in the universe, we cannot help making for ourselves when we think of that grave or revisit it, an image of that friend as dead and decaying in his or her coffin. This image we fasten in our minds, and in so doing we fasten on ourselves the thought of gloom, death and decay. The thoughts of decay and death are things and forces. When we keep them so much in mind we add elements of decay to the body.

We need as much as possible to fasten our thought on life and increasing life--life greater in its activity than any we have ever realized. That is not gained by looking backward. Look forward.

Every regret, every mournful thought, takes so much out of your life. It is force used to pile on more misery. It is force used to strengthen the habit of regretting. It is force used to make the mind colour everything with a tinge of sadness, and the longer you use force in this way the darker will grow the tinge.

Also, when we are ever going back in memory to the past and living in it in preference to the present we are bringing back on ourselves the old moods of mind and mental conditions belonging to that past. This feeling constantly indulged in will bring on some form of physical ailment. The ailment belongs to a condition of mind which we should be done with forever. If we are looking forward we shall shake it off and be better in health than ever. If the predominant mood of our minds is that of looking backward, the ultimate result will be serious to the body.

In the world's business your active, enterprising pushing man of affairs spends little time in sad reminiscence. If he did his business would suffer. His thought is forward. That thought is the real force which pushes his business forward. If he spent it in " sad memories" of the past his business would go backward. He works his success (so far as he does really succeed) by this spiritual law, though he may not know it.

You may be saying: "I have failed in life and shall always be a failure." That is because you are ever leaking back, living in your failure and thereby bringing to you more failure. Reverse this attitude of mind; work it the other way and live in future success.

Why do you say: " I am always sick?" Because you are looking back, living in your past ailments and thereby bringing more on you.

I have heard the expression used: " When the earth was young." As if this planet was now in its dotage and going to decay! In the sense of freshness, increase of life, refinement and purity in every form of life, be that of man, animal, vegetable, and farther on, this earth never was so young as it is today. Youth is life, growing and increasing in beauty and power. It is not the cruder commencement of life.

The so-called "barren rock" contains elements which will help to form the future tree and flower. Is that part of the rock which enters into tree and flower increasing or decreasing in life? It changes only into a higher and more beautiful expression of life. So do we from age to age. The rock crumbles that it may live in this higher form. The old mind must crumble and pass away to give place to the new, and make of us the newer spiritual being. As the old mind crumbles so will the old body, for the spiritual change must be accompanied by the physical change. But if you live in the understanding and spirit of this law you need not lose a physical body, but have one ever changing for the better. As you live in spiritual belief, as the old life goes out the new comes in.

Nothing in Nature--nothing in the Universe is at a standstill. Nothing goes backward. A gigantic incomprehensible Force and Wisdom moves all things forward toward greater and higher powers and possibilities. You are included in and are a part of this Force. There is of you in embryo the power of preventing the physical body your spirit uses from decaying, and the power also of using it in ways which even the fiction of today would discard as too wild for the pages of the novel.

For your spirit youth and ever growing youth is an eternal. heritage. If your body has "aged" that is no sign that your spirit has "aged." The spirit cannot grow old in the material sense, anymore than the sunlight can grow old. If your body has "aged" it is because that body has become the material likeness and expression of a false self or "shell" which has formed on your spirit. That false self is made up of thoughts prevalent around from an early physical age and those thoughts are untrue thoughts. A large proportion of that thought is regret. Regret is an inverted force--a turning of the mind to look backward when its natural and healthy state is to look forward, and live in the joys that are certain to come when we do look forward.

In the new life to come to our race, when we have learned to be ever looking forward to the greater joys to come and cease to look backward and drag the dead past with us, men and women are to have bodies far more beautiful and graceful than those of today.

Because their bodies will image or reflect their thoughts, and their thoughts will ever be fixed on what is beautiful and symmetrical. They will know that what is to come and what is in store for them out of the richness of the Infinite mind must exceed anything they have realized in the past.

Today with the great majority of people their attitude of mind is directly the reverse. Owing to the little trust that they have in that Power the theologian calls "God," they are ever in their minds saying: "There are no joys to come for us like our past joys. Our youth has fled. Our future on earth is tame and dull. It is as dust and ashes."

The truth that life does not end with the death of the body makes slow progress in fixing itself firmly in our minds. The kind of life a man may be living here at seventy does not end in the grave. It continues straight on.

The "old man," as we call him here, wakes up in the other side of life after losing his body an old man still. If he is one of those old men who have "outlived their day and generation," who live in their physical past and look back on it with regret--who have become "too old to learn," and think they have got through with it all, he will be just such an old man in the world of spirit. There is no sudden transformation into youth on the death of a worn-out decrepit body. As the tree falls so does it lie for a period, even in the hereafter.

But in this state he cannot stay forever. He must grow not in age but youth. To do this it is necessary not only that he should leave the old body but the old material mind that made that body. His spirit throws off that mind when he gains a new body (or is reincarnated), and he throws it off because he loses the recollection of all past sad memories and regrets.

The man should in mind be always the boy, the woman, the girl. You can as man or woman be always boy or girl in spirit without being silly or losing real dignity. You can have all the playfulness of youth with the wisdom of maturity. To have a clear powerful mind you need not be an owl.

There may be for a period a certain use for us in going back to our more recent past lives, and for a time living in them. Sometimes we are pushed back temporarily into some old condition of mind, some old experience in order to make us more alive than ever to the rags and tatters of errors in belief still clinging to us.

This may come of revisiting places and people from whom we have long been separated. For a time during such visit old associations, the moods connected with them and possibly old habits we thought long since cast off, resume their sway. We may become for a time absorbed and swallowed up in the old life. We resume temporarily an old mind or mental condition that was formerly our permanent one in that place or association.

But after a little the new mind, the new self into which we have grown during the long absence, antagonizes the old. It feels aversion and disgust for the narrow life, the false beliefs and the dull, monotonous purposeless lives about it. It (the spirit) refuses to have anything to do with the old.

Then comes a conflict between our two minds, the old and the new, which may result in temporary physical sickness. Our old life or self rises as it were out of its grave and tries to fasten itself on the new and even rule the new. The new self rejects the corpse with horror. But through thus seeing the corpse, it sees also fragments of the old self which, unperceived have all along been adhering to the new. We do not get rid of error in belief all at once, and often unconsciously retain shreds of such belief when we imagine ourselves entirely rid of them. These shreds are the remains of old thoughts and former mental conditions. Your new mind so awakened arises and pushes off what it finds left on it of the old. This pushing off is accompanied by physical disturbance, because your spirit puts all its force in rejecting these fragments of the former self, as you might put all your physical strength in pushing off a snake.

Our old errors in belief must be so pushed off before the new thoughts, which come in as the old go out, can have full sway. If your spirit was contentedly and blindly carrying any scorpion of false belief, you would tumble into the pit eventually as so many are now doing. When you live several years in any certain house or town or locality, you make a spiritual self belonging to that locality. Every house, tree, road or other object you have long been in the habit of seeing there, has a part of that self in thought attached to it. Every person who knows you there has in his or her mind the self you make there, and puts that self out then they meet you or talk of you.

If you had years before in that place, the reputation of being weak, or vacillating, or impractical, or intemperate, and you returned to the people who knew you as such, although you may have changed for the better, you are very liable in their thought and recollection of you to have this old self pushed back on you, and as a result, you may for a period feel much like your former self.

You return to such place after a long absence. You have during that absence changed radically in belief. You bring with you a different mind. You are in reality a different person. But the old "you," the old self of former years will rise from every familiar object to meet you. It will come out of houses formerly inhabited by your friends, though now tenanted by strangers; you will find it in the village church, the old schoolhouse, the very rails and fence posts familiar to you long years before. More than all it will come out of the recollection of people who only knew you for what you were, say twenty years before; every such person strengthens with you this image of your former self. You talk with them on the plane of that previous life or self. For the time being you ignore yourself as it now thinks and believes; you put aside your newer self, not wishing to obtrude on your friends opinions, which to them may be unpleasant, or seem wild and visionary; you meet perhaps twenty-five or thirty people who know you only as your former self, and with all these you act out the old self, and repress the new, This for a time makes the old dead self very strong, but you cannot keep this up; you cannot warm the old corpse of yourself into life. If you try to--if you try to be and live your former self, you will become depressed mentally, and very likely sick physically; you may find yourself going into moods of mind peculiar to your former life which you thought had gone forever; you may find yourself beset with physical ailment also peculiar to that period from which you had not suffered for years. Such ailments are not real. They are but the thoughts and wrong beliefs which your old "you" is trying to fasten on you.

I visited recently a place from which I had been absent twenty-five years. I had spent there a portion of my physical youth, and had lived there with a mind or belief very different from that which I entertain now.

I returned to find the place dead in more senses than one. The majority of my old acquaintances had passed away. Their remains lay in the graveyards. But I realized this deadness still more among my contemporaries who were said to be living. They had lost the spur and activity of their youthful ambition. They had resigned themselves to "growing old." They lived mostly in the past, talked of the past "good old times," and compared the present and future unfavourably with the past. They were in mind about where I left them twenty-five years before, and about where I was in mind when I did leave them.

Drawn temporarily into their current of thought "for old acquaintance sake," I talked with them of the past, and for some days lived in it. At every turn I met something animate or inanimate to bring back my past life to me.

Then I went to the graveyards, and in thought renewed acquaintance with those whose remains lay there. So I lived for days unconscious, that in these moods of sad reminiscence I was drawing to me elements of decay sadness.

First becoming very much depressed, I was next taken strangely sick, and became so weak I could hardly stand. I was continually in a nervous tremor and full of vague fears.

Why was this? Because in going back into my past life I had drawn on me my old mental conditions--my old mind--my own self of that period. But since that time I had grown a new mind--a new self, which thought and believed very differently from the old.

The new self into which I had grown since leaving that locality would not accept the old. It shook it off. It was the shaking off process that caused me the physical disturbance. There was a conflict between these two forces, one trying to get in, the other to keep it out. My body was the battle-ground between the two. No battle-ground is a serene place to live on when the battle is going on.

It was necessary in this case that I should look backward and live backward for a season to show me more clearly the evil of doing so. For no lesson can be really learned without an experience. It was not merely the evil of living backward in that particular locality that I came to see clearly. I saw also for the first time, where I had unconsciously been living in the past, and living backward in numberless ways and thereby unconsciously, using up force, which would have pushed me forward in every sense.

I understood, also, after passing through this process, why weeks before visiting that place I had felt depressed, and experienced also a return of certain moods of mind I had not felt for years. It was because my spirit was already in that place and working through this change. The culminating point was reached when my material self touched that locality.

All changes are wrought out in spirit often before our material senses are in the least aware of them. Let no one imagine that because I write of these Spiritual Laws that I am able to live fully in accordance with them. I am not above error or mistake. I tumble into pits occasionally, get off the main track--and get on again.

Power comes of looking forward with hope--of expecting and demanding the better things to come. That is the law of the Infinite Mind, and when we follow it we live in that mind.

Nature buries its dead as quickly as possible and gets them out of sight. It is better, however, to say that Nature changes what it has no further use for into other terms of life. The live tree produces the new leaf with each return of spring. It will have nothing to do with its dead ones. It treasures up no withered rose leaves to bring back sad remembrance. When the tree itself ceases to produce leaf and blossom, it is changed into another form and enters into other forms of vegetation.

I do not mean to imply that we should try to banish all past remembrance. Banish only the sad part. Live as much as you please in whatever of your past that has given you healthy enjoyment. There are remembrances of woodland scenes, of fields of waving rain. of blue skies and white-capped curling billows, and many another of Nature's expressions as connected with your individual life, that can be recalled with pleasure and profit. These are not of the decaying past. These are full of life, freshness and beauty, and are of today.

But if with these any shade of sadness steals in, reject it instantly. Refuse to accept it. It is not a part of the cheerful life-giving remembrance. It is the cloud which if you give it the least chance will overshadow the whole and turn it all to gloom.

The science of happiness lies in controlling our thought and getting thought from sources of healthy life.

When your mind is diverted from possibly the long habit of thinking and living in the gloomy side of things and admitting gloomy thought, you will find to your surprise that the very place the sight of which gave you pain will give you pleasure, because you have banished a certain unhealthy mental condition, into which you before allowed yourself to drift. You can then revisit the localities connected with your past, remember and live only in the bright and lively portion of that past, and reject all thought about "sad changes," and "those who have passed away, never to return, etc." I have proven this to myself.

Is there any use or sense in admitting things to have access to you which only pain and injure you? Does God commend any self-destroying, suicidal act? Grief does nothing but destroy the body.

Chapter 6: God in the Trees: Or, The Infinite Mind in Nature

You are fortunate if you love trees, and especially the wild ones growing where the Great Creative Force placed them, and independent of man's care. For all things we call "wild" or "natural" are nearer the Infinite Mind than those which have been enslaved, artificialized and hampered by man. Being nearer the Infinite they have in them the more perfect Infinite Force and Thought That is why when you are in the midst of what is wild and natural--in the forest or mountains, where every trace of man's works is left behind you feel an indescribable exhilaration and freedom that you do not realize elsewhere.

You breathe an element ever being thrown off by the trees, the rocks, the birds and animals and by every expression of the Infinite Mind about you. It is healthfully exhilarating. It is something more than air. It is the Infinite Force and Mind as expressed by all these natural things, which is acting on you. You cannot get this force in the town, nor even in the carefully cultivated garden. For there the plants and trees have too much of man's lesser mind in them--the mind which believes that it can improve the universe. Man is inclined to think that the Infinite made this world in the rough, and then left it altogether for him to improve,

Are we really doing this in destroying the native forests, as well as the birds and animals, which once dwelt in them? Are our rivers, many of them laden with the filth of sewage and factory, and our ever expanding cities and towns, covering miles with piles of brick and mortar, their inhabitants crammed into the smallest living quarters, honeycombed with sewers below, and resounding with rattle and danger above--are these really "improvements" on the Divine and natural order of things?

You are fortunate when you grow to a live, tender, earnest love for the wild trees, animals and birds, and recognize then all as coming from and built of the same mind and spirit as your own, and able also to give you something very valuable in return for the love you give them. The wild tree is not irresponsive or regardless of a love like that. Such love is not a myth or mere sentiment. It is a literal element and force going from you to the tree. It is felt by the spirit of the tree. You represent a part and belonging of the Infinite Mind. The tree represents another part and belonging of the Infinite Mind. It has its share of life, thought and intelligence. You have a far greater share, which is to be greater still--and then still greater.

Love is an element which though physically unseen is as real as air or water. It is an acting, living, moving force, and in that far greater world of life all around us, of which physical sense is unaware, it moves in waves and currents like those of the ocean.

There is a sense in the tree which feels your love and responds to it. It does not respond or show its pleasure in our way or in any way we can now understand. Its way of so doing is the way or the Infinite Mind of which it is a part. The ways of God are unsearchable and past finding out. They are not for us to fathom. They are for us only to find out and live out, in so far as they make us happier. There is for all in time a serenity and "peace of mind which passeth all understanding;" but this peace cannot be put through a chemical analysis or the operation of the dissecting room.

As the Great Spirit has made all things, is not that All Pervading Mind and wisdom in all things? If then we love the trees, the rocks and all things as the Infinite made them, shall they not in response to our love give us each of their peculiar thought and wisdom? Shall we not draw nearer to God through a love for these expressions of God in the rocks and trees, birds and animals?

Do we expect to find God, realize him more every day, appreciate the mighty and Immeasurable Mind more every day, and get more and more of His Power in us every day only by dwelling on the word of three letters, G-o-d?

You laugh, perhaps, at the idea of a tree having a mind--a tree that thinks. But the tree has an organization like your own in many respects. It has for blood its sap. It has a circulation. It has for skin its bark. It has for lungs its leaves. It must have its food. It draws nourishment from soil, air and sun. It adapts itself to circumstances. The oak growing in exposed situations roots itself more firmly in the soil to withstand the tempest. The pines growing thickly together take little root, for they depend on numbers to break the wind's force. The sensitive plant recoils at the approach of man's hand; many wild plants, like Indians, will not grow or thrive in artificial conditions.

Yet with all these physical resemblances to your own body, you deny the tree or plant such share of mind as the Infinite gives it? No, not that. The tree is a part of the Infinite Mind, even as you are. It is one of the All Pervading Mind's myriads of thoughts. We see only such part or form of that thought as is expressed in trunk, root, branch and leaf, even as with ourselves we see only our physical bodies. We do not see our spiritual part. Nor do we see in the tree its spiritual part.

The tree is then literally one of God's thoughts. That thought is worth our study. It contains some wisdom we have not yet got hold of. We want that wisdom. We want to make it a part of ourselves. We want it, because real wisdom or truth brings us power. We want power to give us better bodies, sounder bodies, healthier bodies. We want entire freedom from sickness. We want lighter hearts and happier minds. We want a new life and a new pleasure in living for each day. We want our bodies to grow lighter, not heavier with advancing years. We want a religion which will give us certainty instead of hopes and theories. We want a Deity it is simply impossible to doubt. We want to feel the Infinite Mind in every atom of our beings. We want with each day to feel a new pleasure in living and, commencing where we left off yesterday, to find something new in what we might have thought to be "old" and worn out yesterday. When we come into the domain of the Infinite Mind and are ever drawing more of that mind to us and making it a part of us, nothing can seem "flat, stale and unprofitable."

We want powers now denied the mortal. We want to be lifted above the cumbrousness of the mortal body--above the pains of the mortal body--above the death of the mortal body.

Can the trees give us all this? They can help very much so to do when we get into their spirit; when we recognize and realize more and more the reality of that part of the Infinite which they express, and when we can cease to look on them as inanimate creatures.

If you can look on trees as fit only for lumber and firewood you get very little life from them. They feel then toward you as you would feel towards a person who regarded you as a thing without mind or sense and fit only to he sawed into lumber or firewood.

When we come really to love God or the Infinite Spirit of Good, we shall love every part of God. A tree is a part of God. When we come to send out our love to it, it will send its love back, and that love--that literal mind and element coming from the tree to us will enter our beings, add itself to them and give us its knowledge and power. It will tell us that the mind and force it represents of the Infinite has far better uses for man than to be turned into fuel or lumber. Their love will tell us that the forests piercing the air as they do with their billions of branches, twigs and leaves, are literal conductors for a literal element which they bring to the earth. This element is life giving to man, in proportion to his capacity for receiving it.

The nearer we are to a conception of the Infinite Mind--the clearer is it seen by us that this mind pervades all things--the closer we feel our relationship to the tree, bird or animal as a fellow creature, the more can we absorb of the vitalizing element given out by all these expressions of mind. The person who looks on trees as fit only for fuel and lumber, can get but little of this element, which to the finer mind is an elixir of life.

The mind which sees in tree, bird, animal, fish or insect only a thing lacking intelligence and fit only to destroy or enslave for amusement, repels from all of these a spirit or element, which, if recognized, would be received or absorbed, and, if absorbed, would bring a new life and power to mind and body.

We get the element of love only in proportion as we have it in us. We can only draw this element from the Supreme Power. We draw it in proportion as we admire every expression of the Infinite, be that expression tree, or shrub, or insect, or bird, or other form of the Natural, We cannot destroy or mutilate what we realty love. The more of these things we really love, the more of their element of love flows to us. That element is for us life as real Is the tree itself. The more of that life we are receiving and absorbing, the more shall we realize a power in life, which can only be expressed as miraculous.

Destroy the forests, and you lessen temporarily the quantity of this element given out by them. Replace the wild tree by exotics or cultivated varieties, and such element is adulterated, and the vigour it can give is lessened. Cover the whole earth with cities, towns, villages and cultivated fields, and we interfere with a supply of life-giving element which the forests in their natural state only can furnish. Keep ourselves dead to the recognition of the tree as a part of the Infinite Spirit, and we are dead and unable to absorb of the Infinite Spirit working in and through the tree.

The trees are always giving out an element of life as necessary to man as the air he breathes. Man's works, as soon as finished, are giving out dust and decay. In our great cities we take in dust with every breath. Nothing in this Universe is still or in absolute rest. Our miles of stone, brick and mortar are ever in movement, slowly and imperceptibly grinding to an impalpable dust. Cloth, leather, iron, and every material worn and used by man is ever wearing into dust. Look at the dust which in a single day accumulates in your room, on shelf and table, or fine garment, even when its windows are not opened. A gigantic ever-moving force is at work there taking everything to pieces in it. Let a sunbeam enter through a shutter's crack and see the innumerable motes floating in it. Think of the myriads of these, too minute to rank even as atoms that you cannot see.

All this is second-hand element which is breathed and absorbed into both body and spirit. But trees and all natural things send out element full of life.

Our bodies also are ever throwing off through the skin matter they can no longer use. In the great city thousands on thousands of bodies are throwing out disused element too fine to rank even as dust. It is thrown off by sick bodies, and many are sick on their feet. This we breathe. We breathe each other over and over again.

This unseen cloud of matter pervading crowded cities is not life sustaining. It has in it a certain life as all things have life, but it is not fit for man's growing life.

When we get eternal life, health and unalloyed happiness, the attitude of our minds will be entirely changed toward tree, bird, animal, and everything in Nature. We shall see that when we really love all these expressions of the Infinite Mind, tree, plant, bird and animal, and leave them entirely alone, they will send out to us in love their part and quality of the Infinite. It will flow to us a new life, and the source of a life of far greater power and happiness than the present one.

"But how shall we live," one asks," unless we cut down the tree for fuel and lumber, slay bird and beast for food?" Do you think there is no other life or way of life than the one we now live? Do you think in the exalted and refined mental condition we call "Heaven" that there will be killing of animals, mutilation of trees and destruction of any material expression of the Supreme Wisdom? Do you think we can grow into that higher and happier state of mind without knowledge of the laws by which only it can be attained? As well expect to sail a ship around the world without knowledge of seamanship or navigation. We are not to drift into Heaven in the way a cask rolls down hill.

We cannot cease immediately from the enslavement or slaughter of tree, bird or animal, nor from the eating of animal food. So long as the body craves and relishes such food, it should have it. When the body is changed by our spirit and belief to finer elements, the stomach and palate will reject meat of every description. It will not abide the taste or smell of slaughtered creatures. When the spirit settles these matters it does so definitely and forever. Man's error in the past has often been that of endeavouring to spiritualize or change himself of his own individual will into higher and finer conditions. To this end he has enforced on himself and others fasts and penances, and abstinence from pleasures which his nature craved. He has never by such methods saved himself from sickness, decay and physical death. He has never by this method regenerated or renewed his body. He has lost his body eventually even as the glutton and drunkard lost theirs.

The ascetic has not trusted in the Supreme to raise him higher in the scale of being, but in himself and his own endeavour. This is one of the greatest sins, because it cuts such a person off temporarily from the Supreme and the life, the Supreme will send when trusted. There is no way out of any sin, any excess, any injurious habit, but through an entire dependence on the Supreme Power to take away the gnawing, the craving, the desire peculiar to that habit. Otherwise the man may seem reformed outwardly. He is never reformed inwardly. Repression is not reform.

The bigot of every age and creed has been the person thinking he could of himself make himself an angel. Such belief makes the man stand still in his tracks. The Supreme is always saying, "Come to me. Demand of me. Find me in all created things and then I shall be ever sending you new thoughts, new things, new ideas, new element which shall change your tastes, your appetites--which shall gradually take away grossness, eliminate gradually fierce, insatiate, lawless desire and hurricane of passion, and bring to you pleasures you cannot now realize."

We shall see more and more clearly in time that when we get the higher, finer and more enduring life (to which all must grow), we shall have the greatest possible inducement to give the trees, plants, birds, animals and all other expressions of the Infinite their lives and their fullest liberty. We shall be compelled to love them. What we really love we cannot abuse, kill or enslave.

We cage a bird for our own pleasure. We do not cage the bird for its pleasure. That is not the highest love for the bird.

The highest love for all things is for us a literal source of life. The more things in the world of Nature to which we can give the higher love, the more of their natural love and life shall we get in return. So, as we grow, refine and increase this power of recognizing and loving the bird, the animal, the insect or, in other words, the Infinite in all things, we shall receive a love, a renewed life, strength, vigour, cheer and inspiration from not only these, but the falling snow-flake, the driving rain, the cloud, the sea, the mountain. And this will not be a mere sentiment, but a great means for recuperating and strengthening the body, for this strengthens the spirit with a strength which comes to stay, and what strengthens the spirit must strengthen the body.

We cannot make of ourselves this capacity for so loving and drawing strength from all things. It is our belonging, but must be demanded of the Supreme Power.

It is natural to ask, "But why did not the Supreme Power implant at first this higher love in us? Why has that power so long permitted man to go on slaughtering and marring nature? Why are tempests and earthquakes and wars and so much in the forces of Nature and the forces of man allowed to go on and bring so much catastrophe and misery?"

We do not undertake to answer for the Infinite Wisdom. It is enough for us to know that there is a road leading away from all we call evil. It is enough for us to know that the time is to come when as new beings with changed minds we shall forget absolutely that such evils ever existed. We shall see in the forces of Nature, be they fire or tempest, or aught else, only what is good and what can bring us happiness. We are not always to be of the material which can be injured by fire or tempest. The fiery furnace did not affect the three jewish children who walked through it, nor was the tempest of any inconvenience to the Christ of Judea when he walked on the waters. What history has shown to be possible for some is possible for all.

Communion with Nature is something far above a sentiment. It is a literal joining with the Infinite Being. The element received in such joining and acting on mind and body, is as real as anything we see or feel.

The ability so to join ourselves with God through His expressions in the cloud, the tree, the mountain and sea, the bird and animal, is not possessed by all in equal degree. Some are miserable when alone in the forest, plain or mountain. These are literally out of their element or current of thought. They can live with comfort only in the bustle of the town or the chatter of the household. They can find life only in artificial surroundings. Their spirits are covered with a parasitical growth of artificiality. This cuts them off from any sense of God's expressions in the solitude of Nature. So cut off they feel lonesome in the woods. Nature seems wild, savage and gloomy to them.

Whoever can retire for periods to Nature's solitudes and enjoy that solitude, feeling no solitude at all, but a joyous sense of exhilaration, will return among men with more power and new power. For he or she has literally "walked with God " or the Infinite Spirit of Good. The seer, the prophet, the miracle workers of the Biblical history so gained their power. The Christ of Judea retired to the mountains to be reinforced by the Infinite. The Oriental and the Indian, through whom superior powers have been expressed, loved Nature's solitudes. They could live in them with pleasure. They could muse by rock or rivulet or the ocean for hours, almost unconscious of immediate surroundings, because their spirits had strayed far from their bodies, and were dreamily absorbing new ideas of the Infinite. You will rarely find a person who as ruler, soldier, inventor, discoverer, poet or writer left his impress on the race, but loved communion where God is most readily found. There inspiration is born. The poet cannot sing of the city laid out at right angles, with sewer beneath and elevated road above, as he can of the rugged mountain wrapped "like Jura in her misty shroud."

We cannot train ourselves to this capacity for enjoyment of the natural things of earth or for drawing strength from them. To assume a virtue when we have it not, is to be forced, "gushy " and sentimentally silly. But when we demand persistently of the Infinite the new mind, which can find and feel God in the forest or on the sea, in the storm and tempest, and feel not only safety, but absorb power and strength, when Nature's forces seem in their most angry mood, that mind with that capacity will gradually take place of the old one, and with the "new mind" all things will become new."

Chapter 7: Some Laws of Health and Beauty

Your thoughts shape your face, and give it its peculiar expression. Your thoughts determine the attitude, carriage, and shape of your whole body.

The law for beauty and the law for perfect health is the same. Both depend entirely on the state of a your mind; or, in other words, on the kind of thoughts you most put out and receive.

Ugliness of expression comes of unconscious transgressions of a law, be the ugliness in the young or the old. Any form of decay in a human body, any form of weakness, anything in the personal appearance of a man or woman which makes them repulsive to you, is because their prevailing mood of mind has made them so.

Nature plants in us what some call "instinct," what we call the higher reason, because it comes of the exercise of a finer set of senses than our outer or physical senses, to dislike everything that is repulsive or deformed, or that shows signs of decay. That is the inborn tendency in human nature to shun the imperfect, and seek and like the relatively perfect. Your higher reason is right in disliking wrinkles or decrepitude, or any form or sign of the body's decay, for the same reason you are right in disliking a soiled or torn garment. Your body is the actual clothing, as well as the instrument used by your mind or spirit. It is the same instinct, or higher reason making you like a well-formed and beautiful body, that makes you like a new and tasteful suit of clothes.

You and generations before you, age after age, have been told it was an inevitable necessity, that it was the law and in the order of nature for all times and all ages, that after a certain period in life your body must wither and become unattractive, and that even your minds must fail with increasing years. You have been told that your mind had no power to repair and recuperate your body--to make it over again, and make it newer and fresher continually.

It is no more in the inevitable order of Nature, that human bodies should decay as peoples' bodies have decayed in the past, than that man should travel only by stage-coach as he did sixty years ago; or that messages could be sent only by letter as they were fifty years ago, before the use of the electric telegraph; or that your portraits could be taken only by the painter's brush as they were half a century ago, before the discovery that the sun could imprint an image of yourself, an actual part of yourself, on a sensitive surface prepared for it.

It is the impertinence of a dense ignorance for any of us to say what is in or what is to be in the order of nature. It is a stupid blunder to look back at the little we know of the past, and say that it is the unerring index finger telling us what is to be in the future.

If this planet has been what geology teaches it has been,--a planet fuller of coarser, cruder, and more violent forces than now; abounding in forms of coarser vegetable, animal, and even human life and organization than now; of which its present condition is a refinement and improvement as regards vegetable, animal, and man,--is not this the suggestion, the hint, the proof, of a still greater refinement and improvement for the future; a refinement and improvement going on now? Does not refinement imply greater power, as the greater power of the crude iron comes out in steel; and are not these greater and as yet almost unrecognized powers to come out of the highest and most complex form of known organization, man; and are all of man's powers yet known?

Internally, secretly, among the thinking thousands of this and other lands, is this and many other questions now being asked: "Why must we so wither and decay, and lose the best that life is worth living for, just as we have gained that experience and wisdom that best fits us to live?" The voice of the people is always at first a whispered voice. The prayer or demand or desire of the masses is always at first a secret prayer, demand, wish, or desire, which one man at first dare scarcely whisper to his neighbour for fear of ridicule. But it is a law of Nature, that every demand, silent or spoken, brings its supply of the thing wished for in proportion to the intensity of the wish, and the growing numbers so wishing; who, by the action of their minds upon some one subject, set in motion that silent force of thought, not as yet heeded in the world's schools of philosophy, which brings the needed supply.

Millions so wished in silence for means to travel more rapidly, to send intelligence more rapidly; and this brought steam and the electric telegraph. Soon other questions and demands are to be answered, questions ever going out in silence from multitudes; and, in answering them, in at first attempting to carry out and prove the answers and the means shown to accomplish or realise many things deemed impossible or visionary, there will be mistake and stupidity, and blunder and silliness, and breakdowns and failures, and consequent ridicule; just as there were ten smashes on railways, and ten bursted boilers in the earlier era of the use of steam, to one of today. But a truth always goes straight ahead despite mistake and blunder, and proves itself at last.

There are two kinds of age,--the age of your body, and the age of your mind. Your body in a sense is but a growth, a construction, of today, and for the use of today. Your mind is another growth or construction millions of years old. It has used many bodies in its growth. It has grown from very small beginnings to its present condition, power, and capacity in the use of these many bodies. You have, in using these bodies, been far ruder and coarser than you are now. You have lived as now you could not live at all, and in forms of life or expression very different from the form you are now using; and each new body or young body you have worn has been a new suit of clothes for your mind; and what you call "death" has been and is but the wearing out of this suit through ignorance of the means, not so much of keeping it in repair, as of building it continually into a newer and newer freshness and vitality.

You are not young relatively. Your present youth means that your body is young. The older your spirit, the better can you preserve the youth, vigour, and elasticity of your body. Because the older your mind, the more power has it gathered from its many existences. You can use that power for the preservation of beauty, of health, of vigour, of all that can make you attractive to others. You can also unconsciously use the same power to make you ugly, unhealthy, weak, diseased, and unattractive. The more you use this power in either of these directions, the more will it make you ugly or beautiful, healthy or unhealthy, attractive or unattractive; that is, as regards unattractiveness for this one existence. Ultimately you must, if not in this in some other existence, be symmetrical; because the evolution of the mind, of which the evolution of our bodies from coarser to higher forms is but a crude counterpart, is ever toward the higher, finer, better, and happier.

That power is your thought. Every thought of yours is a thing as real, though you cannot see it with the physical, or outer eye, as a tree, a flower, a fruit. Your thoughts are continually moulding your muscles into shapes and manner of movement in accordance with their character.

If your thought is always determined and decided, your step in walking will be decided. If your thought is permanently decided, your whole carriage, bearing, and address will show that if you say a thing you mean it.

If your thoughts are permanently undecided, you will have a permanently undecided gesture, address, carriage, or manner of using your body; and this, when long continued, will make the body grow decidedly misshapen in some way, exactly as when you are writing in a mood of hurry, your hurried thought makes misshapen letters, and sometimes misshapen ideas; while your reposeful mood or thought makes well-formed letters and graceful curves as well as well-formed and graceful ideas.

You are every day thinking yourself into some phase of character and facial expression, good or bad. If your thoughts are permanently cheerful, your face will look cheerful. If most of the time you are in a complaining, peevish, quarrelsome mood, this kind of thought will put ugly lines on your face; they will poison your blood, make you dyspeptic, and ruin your complexion; because then you are in your own unseen laboratory of mind, generating an unseen end poisonous element, your thought; and as you put it out or think it, by the inevitable Law of nature it attracts to it the same kind of thought-elemunt from others. You think or open your mind to the mood of despondency or irritability, and you draw more or less of the same thought-element from every despondent or irritable man or woman in your town or city. You are then charging your magnet, your mind, with its electric thought-current of destructive tendency, and the law and property of thought connects all the other thought-currents of despondency or irritability with your mental battery, your mind. If we think murder or theft, we bring ourselves by this law into spiritual relationship and rapport with every thief or murderer in the world.

Your mind can make your body sick or well, strong or weak, according to the thought it puts out, and the action upon it of the thought of others. Cry "Fire!" in a crowded theatre, and scores of persons are made tremulous, weak, paralyzed by fear. Perhaps it was a false alarm. It was only the thought of fire, a horror acting on your body, that took away its strength.

The thought or mood of fear has in cases so acted on the body as to turn the hair white in a few hours.

Angered, peevish, worried, or irritable thought effects injuriously the digestion. A sudden mental shock may lose one's whole appetite for a meal, or cause the stomach to reject such meal when eaten. The injury so done the body suddenly, in a relatively few cases, by fear or other evil state of mind, works injury more gradually on millions of bodies all over the planet.

Dyspepsia does not come so much of the food we eat, as of the thoughts we think while eating it. We may eat the healthiest bread in the world; and if we eat it in a sour temper, we will put sourness in our blood, and sourness in our stomachs, and sourness on our faces. Or if we eat in an anxious frame of mind, and are worrying all the time about how much we should eat or should not eat, and whether it may not hurt us after all, we are consuming anxious, worried, fretful thought-element with our food and it will poison us. If we are cheerful and chatty and lively and jolly while eating, we are putting liveliness and cheer into ourselves, and making such qualities more and more a part of ourselves. And if our family group eat in silence, or come to the table with a sort of forced and resigned air, as if saying, each one to him or herself, "Well, all this must be gone over again;" and the head of the family buries himself in his business cares, or his newspaper, and reads all the murders and suicides and burglaries and scandals for the last twenty-four hours; and the queen of the household buries herself in sullen resignation or household cares, then there are being literally consumed at that table, along with the food, the thought-element of worry and murder and suicide and the morbid element, which loves to dwell on the horrible and ghastly; and, as a result, dyspepsia, in some of its many forms, will be manufactured all the way down the line, from one end of the table to the other.

If the habitual expression of a face be a scowl, it is because the thoughts behind that face are mostly scowls. If the corners of a mouth are turned down, it is because most of the time the thoughts which govern and shape that mouth are gloomy and despondent. If a face does not invite people, and make them desire to get acquainted with its wearer, it is because that face is a sign advertising thoughts behind it which the wearer may not dare to speak to others, possibly may not dare to whisper to himself.

The continual mood of hurry, that is, of being in mind or spirit in a certain place long before the body is there, will cause the shoulders to stoop forward; because in such mood you do literally send your thought, your spirit, your real though invisible self, to the place toward which your power, your thought, is dragging your body head first and through such life-long habit of mind does the body grow as the thought shapes it. A "self-contained" man is never in a hurry; and a self-contained man keeps or contains his thought, his spirit, his power, mostly on the act or use he is making at the present moment with the instrument his spirit uses, his body; and the habitually self-possessed woman will be graceful in every movement, for the reason that her spirit has complete possession and command of its tool, the body; and is not a mile or ten miles away from that body in thought, and fretting or hurrying or dwelling on something at that distance from her body.

When we form a plan for any business, any invention, any undertaking, we are making something of that unseen element, our thought, as real, though unseen, as any machine of iron or wood. That plan or thought begins, as soon as made, to draw to itself, in more unseen elements, power to carry itself out, power to materialize itself in physical or visible substance. When we dread a misfortune, or live in fear of any ill, or expect ill luck, we make also a construction of unseen element, thought,--which, by the same law of attraction, draws to it destructive, and to you damaging, forces or elements. Thus the law for success is also the law for misfortune, according as it is used; even as the force of a man's arm can save another from drowning, or strike a dagger to his heart. Of whatever possible thing we think, we are building, in unseen substance, a construction which will draw to us forces or elements to aid us or hurt us, according to the character of thought we think or put out.

If you expect to grow old, and keep ever in your mind an image or construction of yourself as old and decrepit, you will assuredly be so. You are then making yourself so.

If you make a plan in thought, in unseen element, for yourself, as helpless, and decrepit, such plan will draw to you of unseen thought-element that which will make you weak, helpless, and decrepit. If, on the contrary, you make for yourself a plan for being always healthy, active, and vigorous, and stick to that plan, and refuse to grow decrepit, and refuse to believe the legions ot people who will tell you that you must grow old, you will not grow old. It is because you think it must be so, as people tell you, that makes it so.

If you in your mind are ever building an ideal of yourself as strong, healthy, and vigorous, you are building to yourself of invisible element that which is ever drawing to you more of health, strength, and vigour. You can make of your mind a magnet to attract health or weakness. If you love to think of the strong things in Nature, of granite mountains and heaving billows and resistless tempests, you attract to you their elements of strength.

If you build yourself in health and strength today, and despond and give up such thinking or building tomorrow, you do not destroy what in spirit and of spirit you have built up. That amount of element so added to your spirit can never be lost but you do, for the time, in so desponding, that is, thinking weakness, stop the building of your health-structure; and although your spirit is so much the stronger for that addition of element, it may not be strong enough to give quickly to the body what you may have taken from it through such despondent thought.

Persistency in thinking health, in imagining or idealizing yourself as healthy, vigorous, and symmetrical, is the cornerstone of health and beauty. Of that which you think most, that you will be, and that you will have most of. You say "No." But your bed-ridden patient is not thinking, "I am strong;" he or she is thinking, "I am so weak." Your dyspeptic man or woman is not thinking, "I will have a strong stomach." They are ever saying, "I can't digest anything;" and they can't, for that very reason.

We are apt to nurse our maladies rather than nurse ourselves. We want our maladies petted and sympathized with, more than ourselves. When we have a bad cold, our very cough sometimes says to others, unconsciously, "I am this morning an object for your sympathy. I am so afflicted!" It is the cold, then, that is calling out for sympathy. Were the body treated rightly, your own mind and all the minds about you would say to that weak element in you, "Get out of that body!" and the silent force of a few minds so directed would drive that weakness out. It would leave as Satan did when the man of Nazareth imperiously ordered him. Colds and all other forms of disease are only forms of Satan, and thrive also by nursing. Vigour and health are catching also as well as the measles.

What would many grown-up people give for a limb or two limbs that had in them the spring and elasticity of those owned by a boy twelve years old; for two limbs that could climb trees, walk on rail fences, and run because they loved to run, and couldn't help running? If such limbs so full of life could be manufactured and sold, would there not be a demand for them by those stout ladies and gentlemen who get in and out of their carriages as if their bodies weighed a ton? Why is it that humanity resigns itself with scarcely a protest to the growing heaviness, sluggishness, and stiffness that comes even with middle age? I believe, however, we compromise with this inertia, and call it dignity. Of course a man and a father and a citizen and a voter and a pillar of the State--of inertia--shouldn't run and cut up and kick up like a boy, because he can't. Neither should a lady who has grown to the dignity of a waddle run as she did when a girl of twelve, because she can't, either. Actually we put on our infirmities as we would masks, and hobble around in them, saying, "This is the thing to do, because we can't do anything else." Sometimes we are even in a hurry to put them on; like the young gentleman who sticks an eye-glass to his eye, and thereby the sooner ruins the sight of a sound organ, in order to look tony or bookish.

There are more and more possibilities In Nature, in the elements, and in man and out of man; and they come as fast as man sees and knows how to use these forces in Nature and in himself. Possibilities and miracles mean the same thing.

The telephone sprung suddenly on "our folks" of two hundred years ago would have been a miracle, and might have consigned the person using it to the prison or the stake: all unusual manifestations of Nature's powers being then attributed to the Devil, because the people of that period had so much of the Devil, or cruder element, in them as to insist that the universe should not continually show and prove higher and higher expressions of the higher mind for man's comfort and pleasure.

Chapter 8: Museum and Menagerie Horrors

A Menagerie of beasts and birds means a collection of captured walking and flying creatures, taken from their natural modes of life, deprived permanently of such modes, and suffering more or less in consequence. The bird, used to the freedom of forest and air is imprisoned in the most limited quarters. Its plumage there is never as fresh and glossy as in its natural state. It does not live as long. The captive life of the many species brought from the tropics is very short, especially of the smaller and more delicate species.

Bears, lions, tigers, deer, wolves and all other animals like liberty and freedom of range as well as man. In the menagerie they are deprived of it. The air they breathe is often fetid and impure. To the burrowing animal, earth is as much a necessity and comfort as a comfortable bed is to us. The captured burrower is often kept on a hard board floor, which, in its restless misery to get into its native earth, it scratches and wears away in cavities inches in depth.

Monkeys by the thousand die prematurely of consumption, because forced to live in a climate too cold and damp for them, and no amount of artificial heat can supply the element to which they have been accustomed in the air of their native tropic groves and jungles.

Seals are kept in tanks of fresh water, when salt water is their natural element. Their captive lives are always short.

There is no form of organized life but is a part and belonging of the locality and latitude where in its wild state it is born. The polar bear is a natural belonging of the Arctic regions. The monkey is a belonging and outgrowth of tropical conditions. When either of these is taken from climes native to them, and out of which they do not voluntarily wander, pain is inflicted on them.

Go to the cheap "museum," now so plentiful, and regard the bedraggled plumage and apparent sickly condition of many of the birds, natives of distant climes, imprisoned there. You see them but for an hour. Return in a few months and you will not find them. What has become of them. They have died, and their places are supplied by others likewise slowly dying. The procession of captives so to suffer and die prematurely never ceases moving into these places. Ships are constantly bringing them hither. An army of men distributed all over the world, and ranging through the forests of every clime, is constantly engaged in trapping them. For what reasons are all these concentrations of captured misery, now to be found in every large town and city of our country? 7 Simply to gratify human curiosity. Simply that we may stand a few minutes and gaze at them behind their bars. What do we then learn of their real natures and habits in these prisons? What would be learned of your real tastes, inclinations and habits were you kept constantly in a cage?

Is the gratification of this curiosity worth the misery it costs?

If a bird wooed by your kindness comes and builds its nest in a tree near your window, and there rears its brood, is not the sight it affords from day to day worth a hundred times more than that of the same bird, deprived of its mate and shut up in a cage? Will you not, is in its freedom you study its real habits and see its real and natural life, feel more and more drawn to it by the tie of a common sympathy, as you see evidenced in that life so much that belongs to your own? Like you, it builds a home; like you, it has affection and care for its mate; like you, it provides for its family; like you, it is alarmed at the approach of danger; like you, it nestles in the thought of security.

Yet so crude and cruel still is the instinct in our race, that the ruin of the wild bird's home, or its slaughter or capture, is the ruling desire with nineteen boys out of twenty as they roam the woods; and "cultured parents" will see their children leave the house equipped with the means for this destruction without even the thought of protest.

Chapter 9: The God in Yourself

As a spirit, you are a part of God or the Infinite Force or Spirit of good. As such part, you are an ever-growing power which can never lessen, and must always increase, even as it has in the past through many ages always increased, and built you up, as to intelligence, to your present mental stature. The power of your mind has been growing to its present quality and clearness through many more physical lives than the one you are now living. Through each past life you have unconsciously added to its power. Every struggle of the mind--be it struggle against pain, struggle against appetite, struggle for more skill in the doing of anything, struggle for greater advance in any art or calling, struggle and dissatisfaction at your failings and defects--is an actual pushing of the spirit to greater power, and a greater relative completion of yourself,--and with such completion, happiness. For the aim of living is happiness.

There is today more of you, and more of every desirable mental quality belonging to you, than ever before. The very dissatisfaction and discontent you may feel concerning your failings is a proof of this. If your mind was not as clear as it is, it could not see those failings. You are not now where you may have been in a mood of self-complacency, when you thought yourself about right in every respect. Only you may, now, in looking at yourself, have swung too far in the opposite direction; and, because your eyes have been suddenly opened to certain faults, you may think these faults to be constantly increasing. They are not. The God in yourself--the ever-growing power in yourself--has made you see an incompleteness in your character; yet that incompleteness was never so near a relative completion as now. Of this the greatest proof is, that you can now see what in yourself you never saw or felt before.

You may have under your house a cavity full of vermin and bad air. You were much worse off before the cavity was found, repulsive as it may be to you; and now that it is found, you may be sure it will be cleansed. There may be cavities in our mental architecture abounding in evil element, and there is no need to be discouraged as the God in our self shows them to us. There is no need of saying, " I'm such an imperfect creature I'm sure I can never cure all my faults." Yes, you can. You are curing them now. Every protest of your mind against your fault is a push of the spirit forward. Only you must not expect to cure them all in an hour, a day, a week, or a year. There will never be a time in your future existence, but that you can see where you can improve yourself. If you see possibility of improvement, you must of course see the defect to be improved. Or, in other words, you see for yourself a still greater completion, a still greater elaboration, a finer and finer shading of your character, a more and more complicated distribution of the Force always coming to you. So you will cease this fretting over your being such an imperfect creature when you find, as you will, that you are one of the " temples of God " ever being built by yourself into ever-increasing splendour.

No talent of yours ever stops growing any more than the tree stops growing in winter. If you are learning to paint or draw or act or speak in public or do anything, and cease your practice entirely for a month or a year or two years, and then take it up again, you will find after a little that an increase of that talent has come; that you have new ideas concerning it, and new power for execution.

You ask, "What is the aim of life?" In a sense, you cannot aim your own life. There is a destiny that aims it,--a law which governs and carries it. To what? To an ever-increasing and illimitable capacity for happiness as your power increases, and increase it must. You cannot stop growing, despite all appearances to the contrary. The pain you have suffered has been through that same growth of the spirit pressing you harder and harder against what caused you misery, so that at last you should take that pain as a proof that you were on some wrong path, out of which you must get as soon as possible; and when you cry out hard, and are in living earnest to know the right way, something will always come to tell you the right way; for it is a law of nature that every earnest call is answered, and an earnest demand or prayer for anything always brings the needed supply.

What is the aim of life? To get the most happiness out of it; to so learn to live that every coming day will be looked for in the assurance that it will be as full, and even fuller, of pleasure than the day we now live in; to banish even the recollection that time can hang heavily on our hands; to be thankful that we live; to rise superior to sickness or pain; to command the body, through the power of the spirit, so that it can feel no pain; to control and command the thought so that It shall ever increase in power to work and act separate, apart, and afar from our body, so that it shall bring us all that we need of house or land or food or clothes, and that without robbing or doing injustice to anyone; to gain in power so that the spirit shall ever recuperate, reinvigorate, and rejuvenate the body so long as we desire to use it, so that no part or organ shall weaken, wither, or decay; to be learning ever new sources of amusement for ourselves and others; to make ourselves so full of happiness and use for others, that our presence may ever be welcome to them; to be no one's enemy and every one's friend,--that is the destiny of life in those domains of existence where people as real as we, and much more alive than we, have learned, and are ever learning, how to get the most of heaven out of life. That is the inevitable destiny of every individual spirit.

You cannot escape ultimate happiness and permanent happiness as you grow on and on in this and other existences; and all the pains you suffer, or have suffered, are as prods and pokes to keep you out of wrong paths,--to make you follow the law. And the more sensitive you grow, the more clearly will you see the law which leads away from all pain, and ever toward more happiness, and to a state of mind where it is such an ecstasy to live, that all sense of time is lost,--as the sense of time is lost with us when we are deeply interested or amused, or gaze upon a thrilling play or spectacle,--so that in the words of the biblical record, "a day shall be as a thousand years, and a thousand years as a day."

The Nirvana of the Hindus suggests all the possibilities of life coming to our planet,--"Nirvana " implying that calmness, serenity, and confidence of mind which comes of the absolute certainty that every effort we make, every enterprise we undertake, must be successful; and that the happiness we realize this month is but the stepping-stone to the greater happiness of next. If you fell that the trip of foreign travel you now long for and wish for was as certain to come as now you are certain that the sun rose this morning; if you knew that you would achieve your own peculiar and individual proficiency and triumph in painting or oratory, or as an actor or sculptor, or in any art, as surely as now you know you can walk downstairs, you would not of course feel any uneasiness. In all our relatively perfected lives we shall know this, because we shall know for an absolute certainty that when we concentrate our mental force or thought on any plan or pursuit or undertaking, we are setting at work the attractive force of thought- substance to draw to us the means or agencies or forces or individuals to carry out that plan, as certainly as the force of muscle applied to a line draws the ship to its pier.

You worry very little now as to your telegram reaching its destination, because, while you know next to nothing as to what electricity is, you do know that when it is applied in a certain way it will carry your message; and you will have the same confidence that when your thought is regulated and directed by a certain method, it will do for you what you wish. Before men knew how to use electricity there was as much of it as today, and with the same power as today; but so far as our convenience was concerned, it was quite useless as a message-bearer. lack of knowledge to direct it. The tremendous power of human thought is with us all today very much in a similar condition. It is wasted, because we do not know how to concentrate and direct it. It is worse than wasted, because, through ignorance and life-long habit, we work our mental batteries in the wrong direction, and send from us bolt after bolt of ill-will toward others, or enviousness or snarls or sneers or some form of ugliness,--all this being real element wrongly and ignorantly applied, which may strike and hurt others, and will certainly hurt us.

Here is the cornerstone of all successful effort in this existence or any other. Never in thought acknowledge an impossibility. Never in mind reject what to you may seem the wildest idea with scorn; because, in so doing, you may not know what you are closing the door against. To say anything is impossible because it seems impossible to you, is just so much training in the dangerous habit of calling out "Impossible!" to every new idea. Your mind is then a prison full of doors, barred to all outside, and you the only inmate. "All things" are possible with God. God works in and through you. To say " Impossible!" as to what you may do or become is a sin. It is denying God's power to work through you. It is denying the power of the Infinite Spirit to do through you far more than what you are now capable of conceiving in mind. To say "Impossible!" is to set up your relatively weak limit of comprehension as the standard of the universe. It is as audacious as to attempt the measurement of endless space with a yard-stick.

When you say "Impossible!" and "I can't" you make a present impossibility for yourself. This thought of yours is the greatest hindrance to the possible. It cannot stop it. You will be pushed on, hang back as much as you may. There can be no successful resistance to the eternal and constant betterment of all things (including yourself).

You should say, "It is possible for me to become anything which I admire." You should say, " It is possible for me to become a writer, an orator, an actor, an artist." You have then thrown open the door to your own temple of art within you. So long as you said "Impossible!" you kept it closed. Your "I can't" was the iron bolt locking that door against you. Your "I can" is the power shoving back that bolt.

Christ's spirit or thought had power to command the elements, and quiet the storm. Your spirit as a part of the great whole has in the germ, and waiting for fruition, the same power. Christ, through power of concentrating the unseen element of his thought, could turn that unseen element into the seen, and materialize food,--loaves and fishes. That is a power inherent in every spirit, and every spirit is growing to such power. You see today a healthy baby-boy. It cannot lift a pound; but you know there lies in that feeble child the powers and possibilities which, twenty years hence, may enable it to lift with ease two hundred pounds. So the greater power, the coming spiritual power, can be foretold for us, who are now relatively babes spiritually. The reason for life's being so unhappy here in this region of being is, that as we do not know the law, we go against it, and get thereby its pains instead of its pleasures.

The law cannot be entirely learned by us out of past record or the past experience of anyone, no matter to what power they might have attained. Such records or lives may be very useful to us as suggesters. But while there are general principles that apply to all, there are also individual laws that apply to every separate and individualized person. You cannot follow directly in my track in making yourself happier and better, nor can I in yours; because every one of us is made up of a different combination of element, as element has entered into and formed our spirits (our real selves) through the growth and evolution ages. You must study and find out for yourself what your nature requires to bring it permanent happiness. You are a book for yourself. You must open this book page after page, and chapter after chapter, as they come to you with the experience of each day, each month, each year, and read them. No one else can read them for you as you can for yourself. No one else can think exactly as you think, or feel just as you feel, or be affected just as you are affected by otter forces or persons about you; and for this reason no other person can judge what you really need to make your life more complete, more perfect, more happy so well as yourself.

You must find out for yourself what association is best for you, what food is best for you, and what method in any business, any art, any profession brings you the best results. You can be helped very much by conferring with others who are similarly interested. You can be very much helped by those who may have more knowledge than you of general laws. You can be greatly helped to get force or courage or new ideas to carry out your undertakings, by meeting at regular intervals with earnest, sincere, and honest people who have also some definite purpose to accomplish, and talking yourself out to them, and they to you. But when you accept any man or any woman as an infallible guide or authority, and do exactly as they say, you are off the main track; because then you are making the experiments of another person, formed of a certain combination of elements or chemicals, and the result of that person's experiments, the rule for your own individual combination of element, when your combination may be very different, and differently acted on by the elements outside of it.

You have iron and copper and magnesia and phosphorus, and more of other minerals and chemicals, and combination and re-combination of mineral and chemical, in your physical body than earthly science has yet thought of. You have in your spirit or thought the unseen or spiritual correspondences of these minerals still finer and more subtle; and all these are differently combined, and in different proportions, from any other physical or spiritual body. How, then, can anyone find out the peculiar action of this your individual combination, save yourself?

There are certain general laws; but every individual must apply the general law to him or herself. It is a general law that the wind will propel a ship. But every vessel does not use the air in exactly the same fashion. It is a general law that thought is force, and can effect, and is constantly effecting, results to others far from our bodies; and the quality of our thought and its power to affect results depends very much on our associations. But for that reason, if yours is the superior thought or power, and I see that through its use you are moving ahead in the world, I should not choose your character of associates or your manner of life. I can try your methods as experiments; but I must remember they are only experiments. I must avoid that so common error,--the error of slavish copy and idolatry of another.

The Christ of Nazareth once bade certain of his followers not to worship him. "Call me not good," said he. "There is none good save God alone." Christ said, "I am the way and the life," meaning, as the text interprets itself to me, that as to certain general laws of which he was aware, and by which he also as a spirit was governed, he knew and could give certain information. But he never did assert that his individual life, with all the human infirmity or defect that he had "taken upon him," was to be strictly copied. He did pray to the Infinite Spirit of Good for more strength, and deliverance from the SIN OF FEAR when his spirit quailed at the prospect of his crucifixion; and in so doing, he conceded that he, as a spirit (powerful as he was), needed help as much as any other spirit; and knowing this, he refused to pose himself before his followers as God, or the Infinite, but told them that when they desired to bow before that almighty and never-to-be-comprehended power, out of which comes every good at the prayer or demand of human mind, to worship God alone,--God, the eternal and unfathomable moving power of boundless universe; the power that no man has ever seen or ever will see, save as he sees its varying expressions in sun, star, cloud, wind, bird, beast, flower, animal, or in man as the future angel or archangel, and ascending still to grades of mind and grades of power higher and higher still; but ever and ever looking to the source whence comes their power, and never, never worshipping any one form of such expression, and by so doing making the " creature greater than the Creator."

That power is today working on and in and through every man, woman, and child on this planet. Or, to use the biblical expression, it is, "God working in us and through us." We are all parts of the Infinite Power,--a power ever carrying us up to higher, finer, happier grades of being.

Every man or woman, no matter what may be their manner of life or grade of intellect, is a stronger and better man or woman than ever they were before, despite all seeming contradiction. The desire in human nature, and all forms of nature or of spirit expressed through matter, to be more and more refined is, up to a certain growth of mind, an unconscious desire. The god desire is at work on the lowest drunkard rolling in the gutter. That man's spirit wants to get out of the gutter. Ii is at work on the greatest liar, prompting him, if ever so feebly, that the truth is better. It is at work on people you may call despicable and vile. When Christ was asked how often a man should be forgiven any offence, he replied in a manner indicating that there should be no limit to the sum of one man or woman's forgiveness for the defects or immaturity in another. There should be no limit to the kind and helpful thought we think or put out toward another person who falls often, who is struggling with some unnatural appetite. It is a great evil, often done unconsciously, to say or think of an intemperate man, " Oh, he's gone to the dogs. It's no use doing anything more for him!" because, when we do this, we put hopeless, discouraging thought out in the air. It meets that person. He or she will feel it; and it is to them an element retarding their progress out of the slough they are in, just as some person's similar thought has retarded us in our effort to get out of some slough we were in or are in now,--slough of indecision; slough of despondency; slough of ill-temper; slough of envious, hating thought.

Yet the spirit of man becomes the stronger for all it struggles against. It becomes the stronger for struggling against your censorious, uncharitable thought, until at last it carries a man or woman to a point where they may in thought say to others, "I would rather have your approbation than your censure. But I am not dependent on your approbation or censure, for my most rigid judge and surest punishment for all the evil I do comes of my own mind,--the god or goddess in myself from whose judgment, from whose displeasure, there is no escaping." Yet as the spirit grows clearer and clearer in sight, so does that judge in ourselves become more and more merciful for its own errors; for it knows that, in a sense, as we refine from cruder to finer expression, there must be just so much evil to be contended against, fought against, and finally and inevitably overcome. Every man and woman is predestined to a certain amount of defect, until the spirit overcomes such defect; and overcome it must, for it is the nature of spirit to struggle against defect. It is the one thing impossible for man to take this quality out of his own spirit--the quality of ever rising toward more power and happiness.

If you make this an excuse to sin, or commit excess, or lie or steal or murder, and say, "I can't help it; I'm predestined to it," you will be punished all the same, not possibly by man's law, but by natural or divine law which has its own punishments for every possible sin,--for murder or lust or lying or stealing or evil thinking or gluttony; and these punishments are being constantly inflicted, and today thousands on thousands are suffering for the sins they commit in ignorance of the law of life; and the pain of such punishment has grown so great, and bears so heavily on so many, that there is now a greater desire than ever to know more of these laws; and for that very reason is this desire being met, and these questions are being answered; for it is an inevitable law of nature that what the human mind demands, that it, in time, gets; and the greater the number of minds so demanding, the sooner is the demand met, and the questions answered. Steam but a few years ago relatively met the demand of human mind for greater speed in travel. Electricity met a demand for greater speed in sending intelligence from man to man. These are but as straws pointing to the discovery and use of greater powers, not only in elements outside of man, but in the unseen elements which make man and woman; in the elements unseen which make you and me.

Henceforth our race will commence to be lifted out of evil or cruder forms of expression, not by fear ot the punishments coming through violation of the law, but they will be led to the wiser course through love of the delight which comes of following the law as we discover it for ourselves. You eat moderately, because experience has taught that the greater pleasure comes of moderation. You are gentle, kind, and considerate to your friend, not that you have constantly before your mind the fear of losing that friend if you are not kind and considerate, but because it pleases you, and you love the doing of kind acts. Human law, and even divine law as interpreted by human understanding, have ever been saying in the past, "You must not do this or that, or you'll feel the rod." God has been pictured as a stern, merciless, avenging deity. The burden of the preacher's song has been Penalty and Punishment! Punishment and Penalty! Humanity is to forget all about penalty and punishment, because it is to be won over, and tempted to greater goodness, to purity and refinement by the ever-increasing pleasures brought us as we refine. The warning of penalty was necessary when humanity was cruder. It could only be reached by the rod. The race was blind, and as a necessity of its condition it had to be kept somewhere near the right path by a succession of painful prods and pokes with the sharp goad of penalty. But when we begin to see clearer, as now the more quickened and sensitive of our race do begin to see, we need no rod, anymore than you need a man with a club to prevail on you to go to a feast.

Chapter 10: the Healing and Renewing Force of Spring

Your body is acted on in its growth and changes by the same laws and elements which govern the growth and enter into all other organized bodies, such as trees, plants, birds, and animals.

In the early spring of every year, there comes and acts on this planet a force from the sun which affects all organized forms of life,--trees, birds, animals, and, above all, man. Man's being the highest, most complicated, and most powerful mental organism on the planet, absorbs the most of this power, and will absorb far more in the future, and to far greater advantage than at present, as he learns to place himself in the best states to receive it.

Material science calls this force "heat"; but the quality known as heat is only its outward or physical manifestation. The quality known as heat which comes from the sun is not converted into heat until it reaches our planet and acts on the earth elements. There is little or no heat a few miles above the earth's surface. Were this force in the form of heat on leaving the sun, or during its passage, the air on the mountain tops would be as warm as that of the valleys. As we know, on the highest peaks snow and ice are perpetual, for the sun-force at such elevation is not sufficiently mingled with earth elements to convert it into that degree of heat felt in the valleys and plains.

This force causes the the increased movement and circulation of sap in the trees, which commences as soon as the sun of the new year acts on them. The sap is a new life to the tree, from which later comes its buds, blossoms, and fruitage. The inflowing of this unseen sun-force gives the tree power to draw new supplies of nourishing elements through its roots from the earth. It gives it power also to cast off any dead leaves remaining of the last year's crop which have hung on during the winter, as you may see in forests of oak or hickory.

This force acts also in the later winter and earlier spring months on animals and birds, especially if in their wild or natural state, causing them to shed their last year's coats of fur or feathers. But this casting off of old visible matter is but a relatively small part of the change going on within them. There is also a casting out or shedding of old invisible matter throughout the bird or animal's entire body. It goes off through the pores or other passages in various forms, some visible, others invisible, and is succeeded by new elements within, as the new fur, hair or feather is grown without.

Your body is governed by the same law. During the later winter and earlier spring months, you are "moulting." You are casting off old, dead matter, and taking in new, providing you give this force opportunity to act on you to the best advantage, by ceasing to be active either with mind or body when they call for rest, as do birds and animals during their moulting period, or process of casting off the old elements and receiving the new.

This element or force received at this time by you and them is invisible to the physical eye, as all force is invisible. The new fur, the new plumage of the bird, the new skin and tissues without and within your body, if received, the new buds, leaves, and twigs, are all materialized expressions of this force. They are new crystalizations coming of a new solution of invisible chemicals, in which bird, animal, tree, and your body are bathed. All of last year's solution or elements so absorbed have been used up. The tree or other visible organization of bird, animal, or your body, stands in the same relation to this re-clothing solution as does the slip of metal in the solution of mineral which attracts out of such solution the crystallizations which form on it.

There is no great dividing line betwixt what we call matter and spirit. Matter is but a form of spirit or thought seen of the physical eye. Matter is force temporarily materialized, as in the lump of coal which, when set on fire, sends off the force bound up in it to move the engine. The lump passes then mostly into element invisible. So all about us we find force ever passing from physical visibility into invisibility, and vice versa. Millions on millions of tons of invisible matter may be on a clear day suspended over our heads one hour, the next to fall in the visible form of rain or snow, which a few hours after may be drawn upward again, but invisible.

The Indian called February and March the "weak months," recognizing, as he did, being a closer observer of nature than we, the tendency to sluggishness and inactivity in animal and man, which always prevails when this power is recuperating, and renewing any organized body.

The most perfect crystallizations out of mineral element come of the solution kept most free from agitation. Your body is governed by the same law in this spring renewing and re-crystallization of its elements. To receive the fullest benefit of the heating and renewing element of spring, you should rest whenever you feel like resting, whether it be the middle of the day or the middle of the night. If you keep the body or mind at work against their inclination--if you force your muscles to exertion through mere strength of will--if you work with either mind or body to the verge of utter exhaustion, not knowing how depleted you are of strength until your work is over, as thousands on thousands do and are compelled to do, through our unnatural system of life and the arbitrary demands of "business," you prevent this healing and recuperative power from acting to its fullest extent on the body. You prevent the new element, which is renewing the tree and causing the buds to swell, from assimilating with your body. You hold on to worn-out element which should be cast off as the oak has cast all its dead leaves before the winter is over; you carry, then, this dead element, a "dead weight," about with you, instead of the new and upward rising life. It is this, among other causes, which stoops the shoulders, bleaches the hair, and furrows the face with wrinkles, through shrinkage of tissues.

The decay of the physical body which we call "old age," is owing entirely to man's neither believing nor knowing that he can place himself in the proper conditions to receive a never-ceasing supply of force, which would reclothe the spirit constantly with new material. Mere muscular strength and constant activity of body are not always signs of the most perfect health. In the delirium of fever a relatively weak man may require two or three others to hold him. When this delirium has passed away, he is weak as an infant, yet often, the crisis being passed, is pronounced out of danger. In a manner somewhat similar in the walks of business, in the keen, almost fierce competition of trade, thousands of people lead a feverish, excited life. They are always on a tension. They demand to be in this state. They cannot work unless "strung up" to a certain pitch. If, at times, through nature's own demand for rest, their nerves are relaxed and they feel languid, they mistake this friendly signal for some form of disease, and treat it accordingly.

Even in these cases, when laid for weeks or months on sick-beds, and nursed through what is called a "dangerous illness," and believing it to be one, they sometimes come out at last better and stronger than they had been for a long period previous. Why? Because through this enforced cessation from physical or mental activity, nature was working as well as she could under certain unfavourable circumstances, rebuilding a worn-out body, and as a result the man arose with new, fresh element in his bones, muscles, and nerves, put there because nature had then his body laid up in quiet, so that it could be repaired.

If you will but entertain this idea of spring's renewing force respectfully, though you cannot believe it thoroughly at first, you will receive much help by such respectful entertainment; for if you do not kick a live truth out of your mind when it first presents itself, it will take root and live there, and prove itself by doing you good.

Men, through incessant physical toil, wear out far sooner than is generally realized. The hardy sailor's "hardiness" often lasts but a few years. He is often an old man at forty-five. The toiling farmer, who works the year round from early dawn till dark, and thinks work to be the greatest virtue in the world, is often a mass of bony knobs and rheumatism at fifty. The average duration of lives of hard labour is much less than those given to occupations requiring less physical lugging, straining, and fagging, hour after hour, when the body is really exhausted.

In the mines of California, where I swung a pick for years, and worked with gangs of men, lifting, wheeling, and shovelling, I noted that the last three hours of a day's work of ten and sometimes twelve hours' length, was done by the men, strong as they might be, with far less spirit than the earlier day's labour,--in fact it was often a mere pretence of work, unless the watchful eye of the "boss" was constantly on his men. Why? Because physically they were no longer fit to work. It was only will that was urging muscle to exertion. And of the stout, "hardy" miners, aged twenty- five or thereabout, who were so working in 1860, and who persisted in such drudgery, a large majority are dead, and of those who are alive today, four-fifths are broken-down men.

In the kingdom of nature, we find periods of rest constantly alternating with periods of activity. Trees rest during the winter. The circulation of sap is sluggish. There is no creation of leaf, blossom or fruit. Wild birds and animals after the summer breeding season, do little save eat and sleep. Some animals and reptiles sleep during the entire winter. Even soil must rest to bring the best crop. Where it is forced, through constant artificial fertilization, the product is inferior in flavour and nourishing quality to that raised on "virgin soil." Disease, blight, and destructive insects some unknown to vegetation in its natural state. When man recognizes the fact that he cannot use his body year after year, from the budding strength of youth to the age of forty or fifty under such a full, unceasing pressure of nerve or will power without great injury, and when he does recognize the fact that through placing himself oftener in restful and receptive states, as do tree, bird, and animal in their natural state, he will then, through receiving far more of this element, enjoy a far greater health of body, elasticity of muscle, vigour and brilliancy of mind. He would also have other senses and powers awakened within him, whose existence is still doubted by most people.

Some Oriental and Indian races have, to an extent, the uses of these senses and powers, partly by reason of their more restful lives and their living like tree and animal, more in conformity to the influence on them of the seasons. They have not our domineering, aggressive force, which invades and conquers for a time, as England has conquered India, and our own people have subdued and almost exterminated the Indian. But mark: this force does not conquer in the end. The thought-power which works most while the body is relatively inactive, is really the strongest and ultimately prevails. It is subtle, noiseless, unseen. Working with the highest motive, it refines and polishes the rude, warlike, conquering races, by grafting on them the civilization of the conquered. In such manner was the art and civilization of conquered Egypt transferred to the Assyrian. Centuries afterward the conquered Assyrian transferred this power to conquering Greece. Greece fell before Rome, yet Grecian civilization held sway in Rome. Rome fell physically before the Goths and Vandals, the then savage races of Northern Europe; but in the kingdom of mind it is the influence of ancient Italy which has been the great factor in refining the Goth, Hun, and Vandal of ages ago into the modem German, Frenchman, Spaniard and Italian. Every convulsion, agitation, and conquest has made this power take root on a wider field.

Today the best English mind is seriously studying the laws which at last it has recognized in India, and that force is in a sense to subdue England, for she is already sitting at the feet of India, receiving her first lessons in the alphabet of laws and force, hitherto quite unrecognized by her learned men.

"What power is this?" you ask--"How gained? How developed?" It is the power coming of minds united on one purpose, in perfect concord, and who do not use it all in physical activity. For if you put all your thought or force in the working of the members of your body, in working with your hands at any calling day in and day out, year in and year out, with no regard to the impulses and instincts of times or seasons, you keep all that force working merely the Instrument--the body--and wearing it out. You prevent it from operating at a distance from the body. You prevent also the inflowing and assimilation of this recuperative power of spring. You breed the habit of keeping the body always in motion. You prevent yourself from getting that order of sleep which would bring your body the most strength for the waking hours. For if the body or mind is fagged out day after day, the same order of thought prevails and is fagging it out by night. You breed the belief and error that you are accomplishing nothing unless at work with body or brain. You cannot get into that state of repose when your thought-power could work at a distance and apart from your body, and bring you in time a hundred-fold more of beneficial result than can ever be realized through mere physical exertion.

The quality in the plant's leaf, root, or berry, which, when taken as medicine, acts on the internal organs, is the force in that plant, liberated through the digestive process. The strength you get from bread or meat is force liberated from the food in the same manner. Digestion is a slow burning up of the material taken in the body, as coal is burned in the boiler, and the force freed by such burning you use to work the body as the engineer uses heat to run the engine. The newer the bud, the more tender is its outward material formation, yet that bud, when used medicinally, contains the most active force, principle, and quality of the plant. The choicest and strongest tea is made of the topmost and tenderest buds of the plant. In California, the bud of the poison oak affects some people though they only stand near it, so great is an injurious force it sends out in the air. The tender buds of spring contain that force which, later on, will make the more solid leaf or branch. In your own organization in the spring are the same tender, budding elements. So, if your body is weak in the spring, it is a sign that the new buds, so to speak, within you are forming. They are full of force. But that force has not had time to act on your material organization and form the new bone, muscle, and sinew which will come at a later period. providing such budding or new crystallization be not agitated, disturbed, and possibly destroyed by undue exertion of mind or body, where the same relative damage is done your body as would be done the budding tree by a hurricane.

Possibly you say, "But how can I carry on my business and earn my bread if I so lay my body up for nature's repairs?" We answer, "'The laws of man's business are not the laws of nature. If nature says 'Rest' and man says 'Work,' and will work or must work, man always gets the worst of it." What society calls vicious practices or habits are nor the only agencies which bring disease, pain, and death. Thousands perish annually in lingering agony on respectable beds, and in the "best society." Consumption, cancer, insanity, dropsy, rheumatism, scrofula, fevers, rage are ever raging among the most correct people, from the conventional standpoint. Why is this?

If you are in conditions of life where at present it is impossible to give yourself needed rest and you feel thoroughly the need of such rest, you may rely upon it that your persistent desire, your prayer, your imperious demand that you shall have opportunity to receive and profit by nature's restoring forces, will bring you in some way the opportunity to so profit by them. When any need is thoroughly felt, the thought and desire coming of such feeling is itself a prayer--a force which will bring you helps and take you out of injurious surroundings and modes of life. We repeat this assertion often. It needs frequent repetition. It is the main-spring of all growth and advance into a happier and more healthful life. The Christ of Judea embodied this great law in the words, "Ask, and ye shall receive: seek, and ye shall find, knock, and it shall be opened unto you." He wisely made no attempt to explain this mystery whereby earnest human thought, desire, or aspiration always in time brings the thing or result desired. For this and other mysteries are inexplicable, and so fast as any alleged cause is given for any certain result in nature's workings, do we find a deeper mystery in the very cause.

We say, "wind is air in motion." What sets it in motion, and keeps it in motion? Once we "explained" the tides on the theory of the moon's attraction. But apart from the tides, what power keeps in motion the gigantic system of currents ever traversing the oceans, revealed more fully during the last forty years? What power keeps our lungs breathing day and night, or the blood running to every part of the body? Are not all of these of the power of God, or the infinite spirit or force of good, working within you as it works in everything that lives and grows? Only to us is at last given the knowledge to work this power intelligently. The body of the tree, animal, and bird decays at last, through lack of such intelligence. So, in the past, has man's material part decayed. But this is not always to be. "The last great enemy to be destroyed," says Paul, "is death"; implying that as man's knowledge and faith in the wonderful forces about him and in him increased, he would discover better and better how to place himself in the line of the working of these forces, and in so doing make the mortal part immortal, through incessant renewal of finer and finer elements.

Chapter 11: Immortality in the Flesh

We believe that immortality in the flesh is a possibility, or, in other words, that a physical body can be retained so long as the spirit desires its use, and that this body instead of decreasing in strength and vigour as the years go on will increase, and its youth will be perpetual.

We believe that the reputed fables in the ancient mythologies referring to the "immortals" or beings possessed of powers other and greater than "mortals " have a foundation in fact.

This possibility must come in accordance with the law that every demand or prayer of humanity must bring supply. There is now a more earnest demand than ever for longer and more perfect physical life, because now more minds see the greater possibilities of life. They appreciate more than ever the value of living in the physical. Such demand often takes this form of expression, " I have just learned how to live and it is nearly time for me to die."

The body will grow to these results through a gradual series of spiritual processes, operating on and ever-changing, spiritualizing and refining the material. These processes do not retain the body a person may have now. They retain "a body," and an ever changing and refining body.

All disease (lack of physical ease) or sickness comes of a spiritual process, the aim of which is reconstruction of the physical body, first in the receiving of new elements, and second in the casting out of old ones.

Back of this physical reconstruction, however, there is going on the far more important reconstruction of the spirit out of which is built the body. These processes are continually going on with the body, operating through the skin, the stomach, and other organs, as well as in the periods of physical prostration or indisposition above referred to.

All sickness is an effort of the spirit renewed by fresh influx of force to cast off old and relatively dead matter. But as this intent has not been recognized by the race, the spiritual process or effort with its accompanying pain and discomfort has been held and feared as a signal or approach of death. So with no knowledge of spiritual law, and judging everything by the material, the temporary and necessary weakness of body accompanying the process has been considered an unmitigated ill. Such belief has in the past only aided the spirit to pile on itself more and more of belief in the untruth that after a certain term of years no power or force in the universe could prevent the physical body from "ageing," shrivelling, weakening, and finally perishing.

The body is continually changing its elements in accordance with the condition of the mind. In certain mental conditions, it is adding to itself elements of decay, weakness and physical death; in another mental condition, it is adding to itself elements of strength, life and perpetual life. That which the spirit takes on in either case are thoughts or beliefs. Thoughts and beliefs materialize themselves in flesh and blood. Belief in inevitable decay and death brings from the spirit to the body the elements of decay and death. Belief in the possibility of an ever-coming inflowing to the spirit of life brings life.

If new life is being thus added to you, there must also be an accompanying throwing off of the old or relatively dead matter of the body, just as when an influx of new life comes to the tree in the spring it casts off the dead leaves which may have clung to it all winter.

Through similar inflowing of new life or force does the animal and bird yearly shed the old fur or feathers and take on the new, and correspondent changes take place throughout the whole organization of bird, animal and man.

This spiritual law works in all forms and organizations of the cruder form of spirit we call "matter." In the human being this influx of force is greater than in the lower forms of life. It does not flow equally to all human beings. Some receive more than others. But in the course of advancement men and women are to come who will receive so much of this influx as to be obliged to see these further possibilities of existence, and also to realize them.

When new ideas or thoughts are received by our higher mind or self, they are warred against by our lower or material mind. The body is the battle ground between these two forces, and therefore suffers. As minds come to trust even to a small extent in the Supreme Power and entertain the idea that physical disease and physical death are not absolute necessities, the higher Power must prevail. Some old error will be cast out; some new idea will come to stay; the body will be better and stronger after each succeeding struggle, and these struggles will also gradually become less and less severe, until they cease altogether.

People have in the past lost their physical bodies, because, being in ignorance of the fact that sickness is a process for the spirit to throw off the old material thought and take on new, they have used their forces in the wrong way to retain such thought. They retain it by their belief. Your belief will make your sickness a benefit or an evil to you. If you can but entertain the belief that it is a spiritual process for getting rid of old worn-out elements, you assist greatly the mind in the performance of this process. If, however, you believe that sickness is entirely a physical condition, and that no benefit and only evil comes of it, you are using force only to load down the spirit with more and more error of which your flesh and blood will be in quality an expression, until at last your spirit rejects the body it has been trying to carry, and drops its burden. It rejects at last the whole body through the same laws by which it rejects a part of it when that part is spiritually dead.

If you receive with scorn the thought that your physical body through fresher and fresher renewal of Its substance can be made perpetual, you close to yourself an entrance for life, and open another to decay and death.

We do not argue that you "ought" to believe this. You may be so mentally constituted that you cannot now believe it. There are many things to be in the future which none of us have now the power to believe. But we can if the thing deemed impossible be desirable, pray or demand a faith which shall give us a reason for believing, and such faith will come in response to demand.

Faith means power to believe in the true, or the capacity for the mind to receive true thoughts. The faith of Columbus in the existence of a new continent was a power in him to entertain such idea greater than others of his time. People who to use the common expression " have faith in themselves," have also an actual power for carrying our their undertakings greater than those who have no faith in themselves. When you demand faith in possibilities for yourself that now seem new and strange; you demand, also, the power and ability to draw to you the capacity to see or feel reasons for truths new to you. If you demand persistently the truth and only the truth you will get it, and the whole truth means power to accomplish seeming impossibilities.

"Thy faith hath made thee whole" said the Christ of Judea to a man who was healed. To us this passage interprets itself as meaning that the person healed had an innate power of believing that he could be healed. This power which was of his own spirit (and not of Christ's) so acted on his body as instantly to cure his infirmities. Christ was a means of awakening this power in that man's spirit. But Christ himself did not give the person that power. It war latent in the person healed. Christ woke it into life, and probably only temporary life and activity, for we do not hear that any of the recorded cases of sudden healing in those times were permanent. They fell sick again and finally lost their bodies. Why? Because the faith or power they drew to themselves for a brief time did not come to stay. They had not learned to increase it continually through silent demand of the Supreme Power. Their spirits went back into the domain of material belief. When that belief again materialized a load on the spirit hard to carry, and they were sick, not one was at hand like the Christ to awaken it into a temporary faith or power.

No person can become permanently whole (which implies among other powers, immortality in the flesh) and have entire and permanent freedom from disease, who is ever trusting, or leaning on any other save the Supreme to gain the power of faith. In this respect every mind must stand entirely alone. You cannot draw the highest power if you depend always for help from another or others. If you do you are only borrowing or absorbing their faith. Such borrowed faith may work wonders for a time, but it does not come to stay. When that of which you borrow is cut off, you will fall into the slough of despond and disease again. You had really never drawn from the right source--the Supreme.

Our most profitable demand or prayer made consciously or unconsciously is " Let my faith be ever increased."

When you reverse your mental attitude regarding sickness and do but entertain the belief that it is an effort of the spirit to throw off errors in thought which as absorbed and received from earliest infancy are materialized in your flesh, you gradually cease to load up with error. You commence also the process of unloading and casting out all former errors in thought. The sickness you had many years ago in fear of death has in a sense packed away that particular remembrance of such mood of fear in your being, and with it the belief that accompanied such remembrance. That belief has been working against you all these years as all wrong belief must work against you.

It is literally a part of your real being, as all past individual remembrances and experiences are a literal part of our beings. It is retained in your spiritual memory, although its material remembrance may have faded out. That remembrance is in thought a reality. But it is the remembrance of a false belief, teaching that death and decay can never be overcome. This belief, the reversed action and state of your mind will cast out. But such casting out must have a correspondent expression in the flesh. The physical expressions of all your former coughs and colds, fevers and other illness must reappear, at first possibly severe, but gradually in a modified form. You are then unloading your old false beliefs. But if your belief is not reversed and you go on as before, regarding physical decay and death as inevitable, then with every illness in such mental condition you pack away another error, another untruth, and another addition to the load of untruths, whose certain effect, added to the rest, is to weaken, crush, and finally cause the body to perish.

There is no period in the "physical life" too late for receiving or entertaining the truth. There is no period too late for such truth to commence its process of physical renewal, and though that particular physical life may not be perpetuated, yet the spirit in receiving such truth receives a force which will be of priceless value to it on the unseen side, and by its aid it may be able the sooner to build for itself a more perfect spiritual body, and the ultimate of the relatively perfected spiritual body is the power to be and live in the physical and spiritual realms of existence at will.

If you hold to the idea that mankind are always to go on as in the past, losing their bodies, and are also to remain without the power to keep those bodies in perfect health, then you set your belief against the eternal fact that all things in this planet are ever moving forward to greater refinement, greater powers, and greater possibilities.

Medicine and material remedies may greatly assist the throwing-off process. A skilled and sympathetic physician of any school may be of much assistance. Everything depends on the mind and belief in which you take the medicine and the physician's advice. If you regard both as aids to your spirit in throwing off a load and building for you a new body, you give in such belief great help to the spirit, so to throw off and build. But if you regard both medicine and physician as aids only to the body, and a body also which you hold must at best weaken and perish some time during the next thirty, forty or fifty years, you will load up with belief in error faster than you cast it off, and the load becomes at last too heavy for the spirit to carry.

What causes the man or woman to be "bowed down by age?" What causes the stooping shoulders, the weakened knees, the tottering gait? Because they believe only in the earthly and perishable. The spirit is not earthly nor perishable. But you can load it down literally with an earthy quality of thought which will "bow it down toward the earth with such burden."

It is not the physical body of the old person that is bent and bowed down. It is that part which is the force moving the body, that is, his or her spirit loaded with material thought which it cannot appropriate or assimilate, which becomes so bent, bowed and weak. The body is always an external correspondence of your mind or spirit.

A body thus ever renewing, beautifying, freshening and strengthening means a mind behind it ever renewing with new ideas, plans, hope, purpose and aspiration. Life eternal is not the half dead life of extreme old age.

The person who can see only the physical side and temporary expression of life, who eats and drinks in the belief that only the body is affected by less eating and drinking, who believes that the body is sustained only by force, generated within itself, and that it is not fed of an unseen element coming from the spiritual realm of element, and who believes that nothing exists but what he can see, hear and feel with the physical sense (that is the material which is always the temporary and perishable), draws to himself mostly those forces and elements which cause the temporary and perishable, and these acting in his body make it temporary and perishable.

Death of the body begins with thousands many years before they are in their coffins. The pale face, and parchment-coloured skin, means a half dead skin. It means a portion of the body on which the spirit works the casting-out process of dead element, and taking on of the new very imperfectly. In the freshness of infancy and early youth, the spirit cast out and took on more vigorously. As years went on untruth was absorbed by that spirit. Its growth in knowledge was more and more retarded. Responding physical changes became slower and slower. The body commences to show "signs of age," that is to die. Because such spirit was less and less fed of that element which brings constant renewal of new thought which is new life.

So far does the belief and faith in weakness and decay prevail with the race that wisdom is often allegorically portrayed as an old man, gray, baldheaded, bowed and sustained by a staff. That means a wisdom which cannot prevent its own body from falling to pieces. In that form of being we call the child (a spirit or mind having come in possession of a new body), there is for a period a greater spiritual wisdom than when the child is physically more matured. It is the unconscious wisdom of intuition. It is for a time more open to the truth. For such reason, up to the age of eighteen or twenty, the spiritual casting off and taking on processes with the body are more perfectly performed. These relatively rapid changes in the physical maintain the bloom and freshness of youth. Sooner or later, however, the higher spiritual process ceases gradually to operate. Beliefs in the false, as taught or absorbed from others, materialize themselves in the body despite all the resistance of the higher mind as expressed in pain and sickness. The load of belief in the earthy and perishable accumulates. The body assumes an appearance in correspondence with such thought. At last the higher mind refuses longer to carry such a burden, flings it off, and leaves a dead body.

The death of the body is then the final process for casting off cruder element from the spirit which it can no longer use or appropriate. But it is very desirable for the spirit to be able to keep a physical body which shall refine as the spirit refines, because in such equality of refinement between the spirit and its instrument, our increase in happiness is greatly advanced, and the relatively perfected rounding out of our powers cannot be realized until this union between spirit and body is effected.

When the Christ of Judea said to the elders of Israel of the little child, "Except ye become as this child ye cannot enter the Kingdom of Heaven," he meant as the text interprets itself to us, that they should become as open to that inflowing of force as that spirit (the child) was at that period of its existence. Were such influx maintained, the youth of the body would be perpetual.

The child is more "led of the spirit" than the grown-up person. It is more natural. It discards policy. It shows openly whom it likes and whom it does not. It has often more intuition. It will dislike a bad man or a bad woman when its parents see no evil in that person. It knows or rather feels far more regarding life than its parents give it credit for. But it cannot voice its thoughts in words. Yet the thoughts are still there. It has not learned to train itself to the double-faced custom of the world which smiles in your face and sneers behind your back. It is relatively natural. Its spirit for a time gives itself free expression. When the spirit loses this freedom of expression when we pretend what we are not, when we say "Yes" outwardly and think "No" inwardly, when we court only to gain a favour, when we feel anger or disappointment or irritation within and pretend content and happiness without, we become more and more unnatural in all tastes and desires. We blunt and for a time destroy all the higher spiritual senses and powers. We become unable to distinguish truth from falsehood. We are unable to feel spiritually what faith means, much less to draw this great and indispensable power to us, and without this drawing power the physical body must be cast off by the spirit.

The body in dying does not "give up the ghost." It is the ghost (the spirit) that rejects the material body. Its spirit, through casting off unbelief, becomes more and more accessible to thoughts and things that are true, and, therefore, grows to more and more power, it will, acting in all parts and functions of the body, operate the casting-off process more and more quickly, as it does in the material youth. It will refuse or reject through the physical senses of touch or taste anything which would injure or adulterate it. It can attain to such power that an active poison if accidentally placed in the mouth would be instantly detected and rejected, or it swallowed would be instantly cast from the stomach.

It is not the physical stomach which rejects food unfit for it or casts out the nauseous dose. It is the spirit which moves the organ to such action through a knowledge of its own, that the cast-out substance is unfit for it. It is so unfit because there is no spirit nor quality in the rejected element which can assimilate with and help the spirit. As your spirit grows in power this sensitiveness to all things which can do it evil, be they of the seen or unseen world of things, will increase. It grows keener and keener to the approach or presence of everything evil, and casts it off. It will warn you instantly of the evil or designing person. It will tell you what is safe and fit for your association. It will at last cast out or refuse to receive all evil thoughts which now you may daily receive unconsciously, and which work more harm than anything material can do, for by them the spirit is poisoned.

As faith increases many material aids will be called in by the spirit which will greatly help the renewing processes. These aids will come in the selection of foods, in choosing proper associations and other changes of habit and custom. But it is the spirit which must prompt and direct these material aids. When such prompting comes you will be obliged to follow it. The food to be avoided, you will not be able to eat. Your taste will reject it. The association injurious to you, you will not be able to keep company with. The habit to be changed will drop off easily and naturally.

But if you make any rigid rules for yourself in these matters in the hope they will tend to spiritualize you, you are allowing the material self to take the matter in hand. The material or lower mind is then trying to give the law and rule and refine the spiritual or higher self. Let the spirit increased in faith, do the work, and when the time comes for you to reject any animal food or any of the grosser element in any form, the desire and relish for these will have gone.

In stating our belief that immortality in the flesh is a possibility, we do not infer that it is one which any now, physically alive, may realize. Neither do we infer it is one they cannot realize. Nor do we argue that people should immediately set to work in any material sense in order to "live forever." We hold only that it is one result which must come sooner or later of that spirit evolution or growth from the cruder to the finer, which has always been operating on this planet and on every form of matter. Matter is spirit temporarily materialized so as to be evident to correspondent physical sense.

As we grow in the faith of these spiritual processes for casting out the old and taking in the new, and consequently realize the accompanying greater refinement or spiritualization of the body, we shall aid more and more those who are nearest us in the unseen side of life. For as we become more spiritualized in the flesh they are helped to materialize more of the spirit. In other words, we shall become physically tangible each to the other, because in the material thought we cast off there exists an element which they can appropriate to make themselves more material. Their spiritual bodies are also under the same laws as regards the throwing off and taking-on process. What they throw off as coarser to them is the finer and fit for us, This element we spiritually absorb. It is for the time and condition a certain spiritual food and life for us. Through what they throw off we are aided to spiritualize the body. Through what we throw off they are aided to materialize the spirit.

Chapter 12: The Attraction of Aspiration

Why may we not maintain a level of serenity of mind? Why are we so subject to periods of depression?

It is because, no matter how well-positioned you are in accord with your ideal of living, you are still to a greater or less degree affected by the discordance which reigns about you. Are you gentle and humane toward the animal creation? The wild birds, your free pets who come and build their nests in the grove, are murdered for sport or gain before your eyes and you are quite helpless to prevent it. You live amid a scene of incessant cruelty and slaughter. The animals fostered by man's care are bred under artificial conditions and thereby developed into unnatural and really unhealthy growths for his amusement or profit. This refers to all manner of "fancy breeding." Nature when left alone does best for bird or animal, and the birds or animals have their individual rights as well as man. A strained and morbid taste will grow an enlarged and diseased liver in a goose to make thereof a certain dish. Your race are so growing disease all about you. Disease means mental as well as physical unhappiness. Directly and indirectly this unhappiness affects you.

The finer your organization and the more open is it to a finer life, the more easily annoyed is it here by the many ills about it. You can hardly go abroad without suffering mental or physical pain. Your houses, cars and boats in winter are overheated and full of noxious vapours from the fuel used, as well as emanation from the human bodies packed in them. You may be obliged to sleep in rooms where this unhealthy heat is partly relied on to warm your when at rest. You must breathe it when in the unconscious state of recuperation, and awake with it incorporated into your being. You are liable to eat staleness and decay at the best of your public tables. You are pained by scenes of cruelty, brutality and injustice. That is the predominant thought active in the atmosphere of the crowd, and it affects your thought.

There is thought, or if you please so to call it, mental action embodied in every material thing about you, and the brightness or darkness of the thought depends on the condition of the material thing. The eating of stale fruit or vegetables may indirectly give you the blues. The live fresh fruit gives you life. Decay is the disorganization of matter. You want to feed on the perfect organization, neither over nor under ripe. You want it, if possible, when the article fed upon is at its fullest stage of life, so that you may receive that life.

You violate ignorantly, unconsciously, and even for the time, necessarily, many laws of physical and mental health. Relative to food, air, warmth, as spoken of above, you may always have been dependent on artificial props. You were born so dependent. You may have come into the world with a body, the partial development of artificial and improper food, and an artificial life brought down to you through the blood of many generations.

This artificial life must in some way bring pain. Your alcoholic stimulant brightens for the moment but leaves a much longer period of pain behind it. But the evil of alcohol is really small as compared with scores of causes for human ills in daily active operation about you in places crowded with people, and all the more dangerous from being quite unknown.

You ask, why even in solitude you cannot maintain a certain evenness and serenity of mind of which you realize sufficient to long for?

Assuming that in the past you have been diseased physically, and of course mentally, do you expect to be instantly cured of such a long illness? Certain habits of thought cannot be otherwise than gradually removed. So with certain habits of body consequent on such habits of thought, such as the habit of hurry, the habit of worry, the habit of laying undue stress on things not the most needful for the hour; the habit of trouble borrowing and many others, which permeate and influence every act of life. Their combined effect is exhaustion, and exhaustion is the real mother of most of the ills flesh is heir to.

Whatever exhausts the body, be the motive for effort of good or ill, benevolence or selfishness, lessens the power to resist these many causes for pain and consequent depression of spirits.

So long as earthiness or grosser spirit has the ascendancy, we see mostly on the earth side. We sense mostly the repulsive in the individual. We are slow to see the good. We can like but few. We dislike many. But when spirit gains the ascendancy, this is reversed. We see then clearly the good in all. We are thereby attracted more or less to all. And as we find the good in all, we get good, from all. We cease then to be so strongly repelled by individual prejudices. We love more than we hate. While earthiness prevails we hate more than we love. We see more to loathe and detest than to admire. We are blinded to the good and too sensitive to the evil. Seeing and feeling then more of evil than good, we are injured by it. To hate, to be strongly prejudiced, to be unable to hear mention of the loathed person's name without a thrill of indignation or disgust, is to be continually inflicting wounds on self. To be able to admire, to have the clear sight to detect the good in the lowest nature and to keep the evil out of sight, is a source to us of strength, of health, of continual increase of power. Love is power. You are always the stronger when In a condition of admiration.

Attraction is the Law of Heaven, repulsion that of Earth. Spirituality is attracted to what it finds of itself anywhere. It sees the diamond in the rough, though embedded in the coarsest mould. It sees the germ of superior quality in the coarsest nature. It can fix its eye on that germ, and hide from itself the coarser elements. In so doing it throws its power on that germ, and warms it into life. The basest nature mounts to its highest level in the presence and under the influence of the higher. There is little need for the true missionary to preach in words. He or she exhales an atmosphere of divinity which is felt by all. Precepts need to be felt more than heard. The prejudiced against the sinner is only a spiritual porcupine. He stings all he touches.

So long as we feel that strong repulsion, through seeing only the defects in another, so long are we ruled by such sentiment. We are in fetters. We are in his or her presence so full of hatred as to be unable to assert the better part of ourselves. All our own evil is called out and comes to the front. There is only the clashing of opposing wills. In such case, we, though in reality the more powerful party, become the weaker for the time being. We are obliged to allow the pupil whom we should teach by example to domineer over us. Cynicism is born of repulsion and personal prejudice carried to its extreme. The cynic ends by finding everybody unbearable and at last hates himself. No cynic was ever in good health. Cynicism is blood poisoning. The cynic is ever hunting for the ideal without. He should find it within. This when once found would be ever creating ideals from all without. His own loving spirit would graft and build itself or all with whom he came in contact.

Divinity is also contagious. That would be a poor Divine Plan which allowed only evil to be infectious. Goodness is catching. In good time the world will learn that health is also. But hitherto mankind have so much feared and even admired the devil, as to have accredited evil only with inoculating quality, while all manner of good is supposed to be drilled into poor human nature by painful and laborious processes.

There cannot be the highest health and vigour without aspiration and purity of thought. Pure thought brings the purest blood. Impure thought, despondent, hopeless, repining, fault-finding, fretful slanderous thought is certain to make the blood impure and fill the system with disease. Without aspiration your best care for the body will be relatively of little help. You may as to garb and person be scrupulously clean; you may pay the utmost attention to diet; yet after all you are but cleaning the outside of a vessel which within is ever filling up with uncleanliness.

With an ever increasing purity of thought, cleanliness and care for the body will come as a natural result. The vessel will clean itself. Proper care for the body in all respects will be a loving effort for that body. Bathing will not be an enforced task but a recreation. Diet will be regulated by the natural demand of appetite. Taste or relish will be the standard for acceptance or rejection. Excess will be impossible, so watchful will be the healthy palate to regard the first faint sign of sufficiency as the signal to cease any kind of indulgence. It is this aspiration for the highest and best that in time causes an actual new birth of the body--a total "reformation" throughout in the quality and composition of flesh, bone, blood, muscle and sinews; a change in the material organization corresponding with that of the spiritual. The flesh by it is spiritualized, that is, made up of finer elements. In all aspiring minds is this process going on. The rule of spirit over flesh brings perfect immunity from disease, intensifies every power, gives far greater capacity for effort in any field, and at the close of the Earth life ensures a painless passing out of the spirit--a simple falling to sleep of the earthly body and a waking up on the other, the spiritual side of life.

The path of self-healing lies in the calling for the elements of health and strength, to drive out disease. That is you pray for such elements and they come to you. Strength or vigour is an element of spirit or more refined matter. The more often is your will exercised in praying for it, the quicker will it come. This is the secret for the perpetual maintenance and increase of vigour or any other desired quality. When sensible--by signs quickly detected--of lack of power, call, pray, desire more. Its rapport with the elements causes such power immediately to flow in upon it. You may become weary. Your will put thus in operation causes an immediate influx of strength, as soon as it places itself in certain conditions for such inflowing.

Say you arise in the morning weak, languid, with no physical or mental energy. Keep your mind as much as you can from dwelling on your ailment. Keep it as much as you can on the thought of strength, vigour, health, activity. As aids to erect this frame of mind, fix it as much as you can on illustrations and symbols of Nature's force and power, on storm and tempest, on the heaving billow and majesty of the Ocean, on the Morning Sun rising in all his glory to refresh and invigorate man, animal and vegetation. If there be in prose or poetry any illustrations of this character which affect you strongly, recur to them. Read them, aloud or in silence. Because in so doing you are setting the mind in the right direction to receive strength. In brief think of strength and power and you will draw it to you. Think of health and you get it. Let your mind dwell on weakness, on never getting well, on the dark side, on everything of discouragement, gloom and darkness and you draw to you the contrary and hurtful elements.

As decay attracts and generates decay in the things we see, so does any weak decaying order of thought attract its like of the things we do not see. Unconsciously many sick and ailing people nurse their complaints more than they nurse the bodies carrying such complaints. They are always thinking of them and talking of them. They actually crave sympathy for the hurt more than for the body afflicted with it. And the sympathy so brought out from surrounding friends, actually nourishes the injury and increases the ailment, when the thought of patient and friends should be placed on a strong healthy body for the patient. The more of such thought concentrated on the patient from those about him or her, the more of drawing power you have to bring vigour to the one afflicted.

Bear in mind it is not here argued that such relief can always be immediate. A mind long unconsciously set in the opposite direction of dwelling on self weakness, cannot immediately reverse its movement and set itself in the contrary and strength-drawing direction. It may have become so habituated and trained to dwell on the dark side as to be almost unable to fix itself on any other. But as the attempt is made and persisted in, more and more power will come to put it in the desired strength attracting frame. The effort must be made. It may take time, but every atom of effort so made is an accretion of strength which can never be lost.

Do not demand arbitrarily or despotically that any member of your body get well of a hurt, that any organ or function become stronger. Your body is as a whole an individual separate from your spirit and with a peculiar physical life of its own, as a whole it is an organization made up of a number of other organizations, each charged with a specific duty, as the eye to see, the ear to hear, the tongue to taste, the stomach to digest, the lungs to breathe. All of these are in a sense individual organizations. Each is open to the enlivening, cheering effect upon it of the element called " love" and that element you can send it. Bandage a hurt, lovingly, tenderly and the element not only inspires the careful, tender treatment, but it goes into the hurt. It acts as a salve and a strength. It gradually binds and unites the ruptured parts. Bind it with indifference, bind or wash it as an irksome task and the sentiment inspires not only a careless and even rough treatment, but fails so to salve and strengthen it with the needed element--love. Bind it with actual hatred and you are self-poisoning the part affected. Hate is the element of poison, Love of healing.

The same principle and process applies to the weak eye, the deafened ear or any ailing or weak organ. Will at times your affection direct to the ailing member, and in that spirit ask it to recover its strength. Be not deterred by the apparent simplicity of this statement, but try it. If you are impatient or angry at eye, or ear, for not being perfect in their office, you do but throw that element of impatience on those organs. You fret and annoy them in their efforts to do their best. There is as yet no such thing as a relatively perfected life among our race. Because such a life means a life and a body without disease or pain, and also a life without the present form of death to the body. A relatively perfected life means a life whereby a mind or spirit has grown to, or gathered so much power by simply asking or praying for power; or in other words, setting that mind as a magnet in the proper attitude to attract power, that it shall be able constantly to recuperate or make over the body with fresher, newer and finer material, and also to put this body on or take it off, materialize it at pleasure, as did the Christ immediately after his crucifixion. The Jews had only destroyed his material body. The spirit of Christ had power to re-clothe itself with a new body. Of this another record illustration is the prophet Elijah's translation to Heaven. That which his companion Elisha saw was Elijah's spiritual or finer body, the counterpart of his material body, and this body was of such fine element that it had come into the domain of and could make use of an attraction not yet recognized by our scientists--the attraction or power which draws upward the opposite of the attraction of gravitation which draws downward or toward the earth. The Attraction of Aspiration.

Every thought or desire of ours to be nobler, more refined, more free from malice, ill-will to others, and to do others good without exacting conditions is a thing, a force of unseen element which does actually tend or draw upward, or in other words, away from the earth or any form of that cruder type of spirit seen of the physical eye, or apparent to the body's touch which we call matter. This the aspiring order of thought you draw from the higher realms of spirit or element every time you wish, pray, or desire it. You are drawing to you then, that of unseen element which incorporates itself with your body and spirit, and it then commences literally to draw you toward the realm and element of greater, broader, purer life existent in zones or bands about our planet. It will, as you persist in this aspiring thought, make you stand more erect. The phrase "the upright man" or woman implies that the effect of this unseen element so brought you of aspiration makes you physically as well as spiritually upright. It lifts every physical organ into place. It is the thought current drawing from above the mood of impure or immature thoughts the mood of unwise or personal selfishness which seeks only personal gratification without thought or care of others. The thought or mood of gloom, discouragement, self depreciation comes of the the overruling attraction of earthly seen or physical things.

When you are ruled by the attraction of gravitation, or, in other words, the attraction of material things, it will tend to make your shoulders rounded he and stooping, your head bowed and your eye down- cast. Your heart will also in some way be literally bowed down through grief, or worry, or anger, or some form of immature thought or attraction coming of seen things or cruder forms of spirit. Every organ of the body will be similarly displaced and tend toward the earth. There is always between things and forms material and things and forms spiritual, an exact and literal correspondence. The shape of every man and woman's body, the expression of the face, their every gesture and mannerism to the crook of a finger, and their physical health, is an exact correspondence of their spiritual condition or, in other words, of the state of their minds. It is a duplication in seen matter and movement of what they are thinking in unseen matter.

As you are ruled more and more by the attraction of aspiration, the desire to be more and more of a God or Goddess, the determination to conquer all the evil within you, which is the only way to conquer any and all evil outside of you, your form will in accordance grow more upright, your eye will be more open and uplifted, your heart will be "lifted up," your cheeks will bloom with fresher colour, your blood will fill more and more with a finer and powerful element, giving to your limbs strength, vigour, suppleness and elasticity of movement. You are then filling more and more with the Elixir of Life, which is no myth but a spiritual reality and possibility.

Our race hitherto has been dominated by the attraction of physical things or seen element. It has said there is nothing in existence but what can be seen or felt of the outer inferior or coarser senses, and consequently there has been nothing else to us. A man may perish of thirst surrounded by springs of cool water, and if he know not of such springs there are none for him. Our condition has been analogous to that.

With the more perfected race of the future on this planet there will be no painful death of the body as at present. Every such painful death is the direct result of sin and transgression of the Law of Life. The ending of the body of the future will be the birth or development of a new physical body for which the old one shall serve as a shell or envelope until the new one is ripe and ready to come forth in a manner analogous to the development of the moth or butterfly from the cocoon. Such growths and transitions will take place at lesser and lesser intervals, until at last the spirit will grow to such power that it can will and attract to itself instantly out of surrounding elements a body to use so long as it pleases on this stratum of life This is the condition foreseen by Paul when he said, "O Death, where is thy sting? O grave, where is thy victory?" And again where he writes, "The last great enemy which shall be overcome is Death." We quote Paul, because no ancient teacher has more plainly foreshadowed these possibilities than he. Undoubtedly they were known to others both of the recorded and unrecorded human history of this planet which stretches back to periods far more remote than those inferred in the Mosaic creation.

These truths, these possibilities for avoiding decay, death and pain, and growing into and taking on a newer and newer body, and newer, fresher and more vigorous life, vitally affect us of today. We must not regard these statements as affecting only a coming race of people of some far distant future They affect us. They are possibilities for us. We have belonging to us the powers for bringing to us new rife and new bodies. If you are not told of these your powers how can you ever use them? You are then as a pauper having, unknown to yourself, a thousand dollar bank note sewed up in the lining of your ragged coat. This knowledge is for you the "pearl of great price." You cannot sell this pearl. You cannot trade it for that of your neighbour's. You cannot accumulate your neighbour's powers; you can only grow and use yours alone.

You wonder perhaps and say, "Can these truths, these marvels belong to our common-place age and time? "But ours is not a common-place, or prosaic age and time. It is only our lack of seeing clearly which may make our time seem common-place. We live surrounded by the same elements, and we are in possession of the same powers to greater or lesser extent, whereby the three young Jews passed unharmed through the fiery fumace--whereby the Prophet Daniel, through exercise of the superior force of human thought, quelled the ferocity of the lions in the den; whereby Paul shook off the serpent's venom; whereby the Man of Nazareth performed his wonderful works. " Was not this God's power?" you ask. Yes, the power of God or the Infinite and incomprehensible spirit of Eternal Good working in and through these His children, as the same power can work in and through us the more we call it to us, demand it, importune it and depend upon it. It is simply the power of the higher mind over the lower or cruder mind. All seen element, or as we call it matter, is expression of the lower or cruder mind. Rocks, hills, clouds, waves, trees, animals and men, are all varying expressions of the lower cruder mind. The power of mind over matter means the power of the higher mind over all these expressions of the lower mind.

The aspiration, the earnest prayer or demand to be better, to have more power, to become more refined, will bring more and more of the finer elements and forces; that is spirit to you. But the motive must be the natural heart-felt zealous wish to impart what you receive to others. You cannot call the fullness of this power to you if you intend living only for self. You may get it to a degree and accomplish much by it. Your demand if living only for self may bring to you houses, wealth and fame. But the demand based on the selfish motive will in the end bring only pain, disease and disappointment.

Chapter 13: The Accession of New Thought

New thought is new life. When an invention, a discovery first breaks on the inventor's mind, it fills him with joy. The blood in his veins surges with a fresher impetus. The author or poet is lifted into ecstasy of emotion by a new conception; I mean the relatively few creative authors and poets--not the many who, borrowing the fire of Genius, put it in their own lanterns and pass it off, often successfully as their own.

"A piece of good news," as we term it in a period of gloom, depression, discouragement; the possible realization of a hope, the removal of an ill or danger, is but a thought after all--is but the picture in the mind of the thing desired--is not the thing itself, yet how it brings strength to the whole body.

An entertaining spectacle, a drama so perfectly acted as to absorb all one's attention, an interview with one to whom we are strongly attracted, a pursuit, or exercise, or art, which interests and fascinates--all these are as food and nourishment, stimulation to the body, and in the absorbtion or excitement of the moment, hunger for material food may pass away or be forgotten.

So we do not live by bread alone. But our natures demand ever new and newer food of thought. The play so charming when first seen may become tiresome through repetition. The air so fascinating when first heard, becomes worn through familiarity. There may even be longed for, a change from the quality of the thought of the mind most attractive to us.

I mean for all these a change, but only for a time. The play, the opera, the artist may in time be seen again and with increase of pleasure, either from the influence of former association, or from new growths and shadings in the artist's rendering, or from new capacity in ourselves to see what we could not see before. Call, then, all new thought, and if you please new emotion, food--food as necessary to make the relatively perfect physical and mental man or woman as is the bread we eat. We desire ever fresh food; we similarly desire and need always new and fresh thought.

Old thought--constant repetition of the same thought--involves decay, sluggishness of mind, sluggishness of body.

Suppose that we rose each morn with the absolute certainty that each day was to be a day involving to us more or less of the excitement of discovery in something useful and enjoyable, and also of similar use to others--something endurable for us and others--endurable for eternity--some unexpected branching out of yesterday's truth, which for yesterday seemed fully grown--something telling us how life may be made still fuller of durable and harmless enjoyment; some great law principle in Nature recognized possibly for the first time in some heretofore called "little thing," in the fall of a leaf, in the colouring of a leaf by the autumnal frost, in its almost equal vividness of colour coming through the heat of Spring.

What must be the pleasure to an open and receptive mind to find today an increase of improvement in the quality almost despaired of yesterday--an increase of patience in doing the perplexing work --an increase of courage--an increase of perception to see beauty in what yesterday it passed by with indifference--an increase of power to control unruly appetite--an increase of power to drive away unpleasant and therefore injurious thought.

Would not such be encouraging, cheering, life giving, health-giving thoughts? This order and accession of ever new thought knows no stop in any direction. It says: "Are you orderly today? You will find some power and room and capacity to be more orderly tomorrow. "Was your last effort in music, in painting, in composition, in acting, in oratory, your greatest triumph?" "You will find some way of making it more perfect tomorrow." That will take nothing from the last effort. It is only a more beautiful and delicate tint for some already beautiful picture. The consciousness of such never-ending growth of improvement is also food for the growing mind, other than bread. Yet it is bread. It is the "Bread of Life," and to be desired as "Our Daily Bread."

Would not also the thought each morning that a Great Power, an infinitely wise mind, was always ready to give more knowledge to help you through troubles--troubles from without and troubles from within. Would not such thought, and the trust begotten of it, be as food, strength, and healthy stimulation?

Especially when the reality of this Power and its ability to aid had been proven to you many times, so that the hope had become a conviction? Grant that new thought is healthy stimulation and also a necessary food to a more perfected life and the question arrives, "How shall we get it?" In other words, "How may we attune ourselves or how may we become more receptive to all that is beautiful and useful in Nature?" For in our religion the useful always implies the beautiful. It is almost farcical to answer, "Live a pure life." That implies so much; so much in so many cases to be done; so much of inherent tendency to be outgrown; so many difficulties to be met; so many conditions necessary for such life so difficult to make. The desire for accumulation seems a Law of our Natures. In its cruder working it accumulates money: in its higher form it would accumulate powers and qualities of mind. "I am $100 or $500 richer than I was this morning," says, with satisfaction and pleasure at night, the money accumulator. That pleasant thought is to him a bit of the bread of Life--but not of enduring life, or in the end, if at all healthy life.

"I," may say another man at night, "am richer than I was this morning by so much more patience, by a bit more of skill or dexterity in my art, by certain knowledge of which I knew nothing twenty four hours ago."

Are we yet fully awakened to the thought that we are receptacles for thought and with thought knowledge, and with knowledge Power, and that our capacity for receiving all these may be limitless, and that the supply of knowledge, power, new thought in the Universe is limitless also, and that it is all ours to draw from, and that the Bank can no more break than Eternity can end.

There are thousands of things, events and scenes in your past life which it is more profitable to forget than to remember. By so forgetting you allow entrance for new idea, which is new life. By remembering you prevent the coming to you of such new idea and life.

By "forgetting," I mean that you should avoid living in unpleasant past scenes and remembrances. Absolutely to forget or wipe out completely from memory anything it has once taken note of is impossible. For everything you have seen, learned, sensed or heard is stored away, and is capable under certain circumstances of being brought to view again.

In place of the term forgetting it would be better to say you should cultivate the power of driving from your mind and putting out of sight whatever makes you feel unhappy or whatever you discover that is unprofitable to remember.

It is impossible absolutely to wipe out anything your memory has once written on its tablets, for whatever the scene, event or experience may have been, it has become a part of your real self or spirit. In other words your spirit is made up of all its experiences and consequent remembrances extending to an infinite past. Of these some are vivid, some vague, and much is buried out of present sight, but capable under certain circumstances of being called to remembrance. To destroy such remembrance, if possible, would be to destroy so much of your mind.

All experiences are valuable for the wisdom they bring or suggest. But when you have once gained wisdom and knowledge from any experience, there is little profit in repeating it, especially if it has been unpleasant, You do actually repeat it when you remember it or live it over again in thought. This is what people are doing who brood over past misfortunes and disappointments.

It is what people are doing when they recall with regret their youth as bright and joyous as compared with the gloom of their middle or old age. Live in the pleasant remembrance of your youth, if you so desire. That will do you good. But do not set it in its brightness and freshness against a dark background of the present. Do not think of it in that vein.

Remember that the time of your infancy and youth, with all its freshness and newness, was also the time of some other people's old age when the world seemed stale and joyless, when to them all that life seemed capable of yielding seemed exhausted, when nothing seemed to remain but to wither and die. Remember also that today if the world seems less bright than formerly, if the sun seems setting instead of rising, it seems now to the boy and girl of ten or fifteen as it did to you at that age.

No person could hold his or her physical body and enjoy life who as they lived on lived in the past and refused to set or open their minds to the future. In so doing they accumulate more and more of the old and relatively lifeless thought, and this element materializes itself on the body. Their flesh, bone and blood then become an actual expression of the dead and inert spirit.

To live carrying such an ever-increasing load must result only in weakness and misery so long as the spirit can carry it. But the mind rejecting the old which it has no use for and ever pressing on to the new, adds the new thought to itself, and this newness of idea will materialize a newer body.

You do actually make the "things before " pleasant or unpleasant for you according as you think of them in advance.

There is a class of people who, if in difficulties and anyone suggests a way out, instantly raise objections and find difficulties in the plan proposed. When in thought we so find difficulties, we actually make them. To lay awake nights and brood, devise, turn over or invent possible coming troubles is force and industry ill employed in preparing the way for those troubles.

In all business we must press on in mind to the successful result. We must see in mind or imagination the thing we plan completed, the system or method organized and in working order, the movement or undertaking advancing and ever growing stronger and more profitable. To spend time and force in looking back and living past troubles or obstacles over again, and out of such living and mental action to conjure more difficulties or oppositions, is literally to spend time and force in destroying your undertaking, or in manufacturing obstacles to put in your own way.

Forgetting the things behind and pressing on to those before is a maxim having a thousand intensely practical applications. Every business success is founded on it.

Men who cease to live in old methods and press forward to new, achieve the greatest financial success. But men who having started out during their physical youth with the new, allow themselves with advancing years to hold on to what was new in their youth, but which is relatively old now, are really on the back track. Money may continue to pour in upon them, but their methods are really out of date, and a few more years will see their business superseded by the newer system.

If you were debilitated, weak or sick yesterday at any hour, do not commence today with living in thought in the same weakness or debility at that hour. Forget it, live away from it, and press onward to the thought of being strong, well and vigorous at that hour.

When you in mind look behind and live behind the thought of the sickness, weakness or indisposition of yesterday, you are actually making the conditions for having the same physical troubles. When you at the day's commencement in thought look before to the new thing, the thought of health and strength at the time your lack of vigour commenced, you are making the conditions for realizing such health and strength.

If it does not come the first day of such trial, try the next, and the next after that. The state you seek will come in time.

Perhaps you say to me in mind: But how can you prove these assertions? They have not been realized in our time. "Decay and death at last overtake all"

You can commence yourself to prove them. If you experiment with any of the methods here suggested for working thought to profitable result and you prove for yourself ever so little, you must thereby gain some faith in this law. If the law is by you proven a little, is it unreasonable to say it will prove more if followed in this direction?

Unreasoning prejudices are bred out of this continual living in the past. The man of sixty or seventy often lives in moods, usages and customs peculiar to his youth. He accepts these as the most fit and proper thing for him. He would probably regard with disfavour and prejudice the man who at his daily business should wear the knee breeches, stockings, waistcoat, ruffled shirt and cocked hat of the eighteenth century. Yet such style was common one hundred years ago. His great-grandfather probably wore such a suit. Yet his great-grandfather would probably have regarded with the same disfavour and prejudice the man dressed in the fashion of today. So a few years relatively have begotten these two unreasoning prejudices with the great-grandfather and great-grandson, founded only on the fact that they were fashions peculiar to the youth of each.

It is, of course, impossible for a person to fly in the face of popular custom or usage--to dress differently or in certain ways live differently without bringing on him unpleasant and even injurious results. For the action of many minds sending toward you ever the thought of prejudice, dislike or ridicule would tend to injure mind and body.

But the sentiment which sends this kind of thought toward another, who departs from any established custom, when that person thereby affects no one's peace or comfort, is a gross error. It is an unreasoning mental tyranny which so regards with hostile mind a man who, e.g., should today adopt the costume of the ancient Greeks--a garb, by the way, more sensible and comfortable than ours.

Less than two hundred years ago such a sentiment mobbed the man in England who carried the first umbrella. This sentiment comes of that fossilized condition of mind which persists in living in the things that are behind and averts itself from such as are before.

Life is a continual advance forward. If we are advancing forward, it is better to look forward. And all are advancing, even the dullest, the grossest, and most perverse. A mighty, eternal and incomprehensible force pushes us all forward. But while all are so being pushed, many linger and look back. Unconsciously, they oppose this force. So to do is to court evil, pain, disease and distress.

Whatever the mind is set upon, or whatever it keeps most in view, that it is bringing to it, and the continual thought or imagining must at last take form and shape in the world of seen and tangible things.

I repeat this assertion often in these books and in various forms of expression because this fact is the cornerstone of your happiness or misery, permanent health and prosperity, or poverty. It needs to be kept as much as possible in mind. Our thought is the unseen magnet, ever attracting its correspondence in things seen and tangible. As we realize this more and more clearly, we shall become more and more careful to keep our minds set in the right direction. We shall be more and more careful to think happiness and success instead of misery and failure. It is very wonderful that the happiness or misery of our lives should be based on what seems so simple a law and method. But so-called "simple" things in Nature on investigation generally turn out incomprehensible and ever deepening mysteries. What most concerns us is to know a cause or agency that will produce a given result. When we realize that we can and do think ourselves into what we are, as regards health, wealth and position, we realize also that we have found in ourselves "the pearl of great price," and we hasten to tell our neighbour that he may seek and find in himself this pearl and power also, for no one is made poorer through his finding that which can belong to him alone, and all are made richer and happier as each finds his or her pearl, through the power it gives them to add to the general wealth and happiness.

Life is fuller of possibilities for pleasure than has ever been realized. The real life means a perpetual and ever increasing maturity. It means the preservation of the physical body, so that it can be used on this stratum of existence whenever the spirit desires to use it. It means the preservation of that body, not only free from pain and sickness, but free from the debility, weakness and decay of what we call "old age," which is in reality only the wearing out of the instrument used by the spirit for lack of knowledge to ever recuperate and regenerate it.

Life means the development in us of powers and pleasures which fiction in its highest flights has never touched. It means an ever-increasing freshness, an ever-increasing perception and realization of all that is grand, wonderful and beautiful in the universe, a constantly increasing discovery of more and more that is grand, beautiful and wonderful, and a constantly increasing capacity for the emotional part of our natures to sense such happiness. Life is eternal in the discovery and realization of these joys. Their source is inexhaustible. Their quality and character must be unknown until they reach us. In the words of the Apostolic record, "Eye hath not seen nor ear heard, neither have entered into the heart of man the things which God hath prepared for them that love Him."

In so-called ordinary things we get out of our lives and our senses but the merest fragment of the pleasure they can be made capable of giving us. Our food is capable of giving far more pleasure to the sense of taste than it may now. We do not get nearly as much pleasure from the ear and eye as they are capable of giving. With bodies more highly developed and refined, food when taken into the stomach should act as a healthy stimulant and give that impulse, vigour and bounding life which it gives to the young animal. The movement of every muscle, as in walking, can be made to give pleasure.

Through following the Spiritual Law, that peace of mind "which passeth all understanding" is in the future to come to many. That it has not in the past been realized is no proof it will not be. Life, then, whether its forces are in activity or at rest, will ne perpetual Elysium.

But millions of our race do not look forward to such joyous possibilities at all. They have never heard of them. The great majority would not believe did they hear of them. They press on in mind to what?

To a belief which grows stronger with years that life is short, that old age and decay are absolute certainties and must come to all, that at a certain age of the body its powers must decrease, and that as weak and feeble old men and women now are before their eyes, so, in time, they must be, and that one great aim of life should be to lay up a store of money to "provide for old age."

These are not pleasant things to contemplate. The many do not contemplate them. They shut their eyes to these gloomy views of their future, but they believe in them just the same. They believe and dread. If they believe, they must in mind press on to such belief. It is this pressing forward that makes of the thing believed in, a material or physical reality.

"Providing for old age" makes the old age of the body, because the person so "providing" sees him or herself for years as helpless and decrepit. What the mind so projects for the future it is making for the future. A material thing (money) is relied on to secure one from ills, when all material things are quite powerless to prevent such ills. The rich man with an aged, worn, diseased body can only buy with his money a better room and bed to live in than the poor man. His money does not prevent disease and weakness. It cannot give him an appetite for the costliest food. In pain and anguish the Emperor is in all respects on the same level with the pauper, for in extreme misery a soft bed and numerous attendants give little or no comfort.

Now in all this, thought element worked in ignorance in the wrong direction proves that it brings a result, but a woeful one. It is only the cultivation of the power of the spirit over the body that can prevent these ills. That power we first begin to cultivate and increase when we come to recognize and believe that mind or spirit is the power governing our bodies, and that whatever mind persistently images, thinks or imagines, it makes. Now, unconsciously, we image in the wrong direction. We think the old age or wearing out of the body must be, because, so far as we know, it always has been. We press on in imagination and unwelcome belief to gloom and physical decay. We hold these sad pictures ever in our minds. Having no faith in the brighter view, we do not look toward that view to life, and ever increasing life.

In the New Testament (the last revelation) we find the Christian and Apostolic teaching full of the sentiment of life, and life everlasting. Death is not argued or implied as an absolute necessity, but as an "enemy" which is ultimately to be destroyed.

It was never said or implied that the advent of "greater revelations" was not to be until millions on millions of years in the future. The dawn of such advent may be now. It is now, not because of any one man's writings or assertions, but because many minds are now open to the reception of the greater revelation, which for centuries has been knocking at humanity's door, but could not enter by reason of the obtuseness and dull ear of those whom it sought to arouse and benefit.

The only dead people in the Universe are the spiritually dead, those "dead in trespasses and sins" who have not as yet learned to forget or rather to refuse to live in and depend on the relatively dead or inert element of earth instead of that drawn from a higher source.

Still the few in the vanguard pressing onward are crying out: "Why, here under our noses is the greatest of all motive powers! Why, human thought is a real element, a real force, darting out like electricity from every man's or woman's mind, injuring or relieving, killing or curing, building fortunes or tearing them down, working for good or ill, every moment, night or day, asleep or awake, carving, moulding and shaping people's faces and making them ugly or agreeable.

Before you give so much of your thought to others, ask. in view of these possibilities, if some is not due to yourself. If you can build yourself up into a living power--if you can, with others, prove that physical health and vigour can take the place of old age--that all disease can be banished from the body--that material riches and necessities can come of laws and methods not now generally practised, and that life is not the short, unsatisfactory, hopeless thing which at the best it now is, will you not to the world at large do a thousand-fold more good than if you expended your thought in feeding a few hungry mouths or relieving a few physical necessities of others?

Our richest men, our rulers, our famous men in art, science and war, our professors, our ministers, our greatest successes, what is their end? Weakness decay and disease. Our more thoughtful people admit that by the time they have learned something of life, it is time to die. The obituary from the living is at best an apology for the unsatisfactory ending of a human life.

Mankind demand something better. That demand, that cry has been swelling and increasing in volume for many centuries. Demand must always be answered. This demand is now being answered, first to the few, next to the many. New light, new knowledge and new results in human life and all it involves, are coming to this earth.

www.ingramcontent.com/pod-product-compliance
Lightning Source LLC
LaVergne TN
LVHW011329080426
835513LV00006B/260